W. Owen
Head of Business Studies Department,
Exeter College of Further Education

A. R. Leal
Chief Examiner for Background to Business in the
Secretarial Studies Certificate of the London
Chamber of Commerce and
Head of Business Studies Department,
Plymouth College of Further Education

Background to business

Longman London and New York

Longman Group Limited,
Longman House,
Burnt Mill, Harlow, Essex, U.K.

*Published in the United States of America
by Longman Inc., New York*

© Longman Group Limited 1979

First published 1979
Second impression 1980

British Library Cataloguing in Publication Data

Leal, Andrew Richard
    Background to business. — (Longman secretarial
    studies series).
    1. Commerce
    I. Title   II. Owen, W
    380   HF1007   78-41319

    ISBN 0-582-41180-7

Printed in Great Britain by
Richard Clay (The Chaucer Press) Ltd, Bungay, Suffolk

Longman Secretarial Studies Series

Series Editor
A. R. Leal
*Head of Business Studies Department,
Plymouth College*

Titles in the series
Assignments in communication   *J. F. Purkis*
Background to business   *W. Owen and A. R. Leal*
Progressive transcription development   *M. Quint*
Progressive typewriting assignments
                    M. Quint and A. Edwards

Related titles also published by Longman
The Office Books 1 and 2   *M. Pincott*

Series foreword

I am more than pleased to note that the increasing popularity of the secretarial examinations of the London Chamber of Commerce and Industry, Commercial Education Scheme, has led to a publisher feeling justified in launching a series of books specifically designed to meet our syllabus requirements.

In 1956 the Commercial Education Scheme introduced a comprehensive and progressive scheme of secretarial qualifications which now range from the Secretarial Studies Certificates, through the Private Secretary's Certificate, to the high levels of the Private Secretary's Diploma. The standards were set high, but were a realistic interpretation of the demands by employers of their employees at different points in their careers. The success of this policy is seen in the increasing numbers of candidates from centres in the UK and overseas and with the very considerable public recognition by Press, Radio and Television when the Secretary of the Year Award is announced on the basis of the candidate achieving the best all-round success in the Private Secretary's Diploma.

May I wish all potential students every success, and hope that they and their teachers will find considerable help in this book.

R. W. Cattell, MA, FESB, MBIM
Director of the Commercial Education Scheme
London Chamber of Commerce and Industry.

Preface

Teaching the Background to Business syllabus of the Secretarial Studies Certificate has often posed problems because no specialist textbook existed which fully covered the syllabus. Existing commerce books ignored areas such as Communications, Collective Bargaining and Training, whilst containing topics outside the syllabus. After repeated requests we have written a book specifically for this syllabus. The examiner has expanded the often vague syllabus and the chapters cover all the relevant material in sufficient detail. Some areas may be less fully dealt with than in existing commerce textbooks but this reflects the differing requirements of the secretarial examination.

Each chapter ends with a list of past examination questions, and where the chapter content was introduced to the examination in 1979 the examiner has included sample questions.

The authors would like to thank their wives and their students who helped to validate the material. Any errors or omissions are, however, entirely their responsibility.

Contents

Acknowledgement

The authors would like to thank the London Chamber of Commerce for permission to quote questions from past examination papers.

The publishers are indebted to the following for permission to reproduce copyright material:
Her Majesty's Stationery Office for a table from *Annual Abstract of Statistics*; Organisation for Economic Co-operation and Development, Paris, for a table from *National Accounts OECD*.

Trade unions and their objectives

Chapter 1

The form of association known as a **trade union** occurs when a group of employees join together and collectively bargain for their wages and other conditions of employment with their employers.

History

Although combinations of workers can be traced back to mediaeval times, it was the Industrial Revolution and the development of the factory system in the nineteenth century which led to the significant growth of the British Trade Union Movement. The individual worker in the nineteenth century found himself in a weak position to challenge the low pay and appalling working conditions offered by the factory owner. The growth of the 'Factory System' and the 'Machine Age' gave the latter the power to replace any individual who challenged the system. It was gradually realised this power could be challenged by employees if they organised themselves into trade unions and bargained as a collective group, sometimes withdrawing their labour, or using other sanctions, if their demands were not met.

Today over 50 per cent of the working population are trade union members and, through the Trades Union Congress (T.U.C.), trade unions are involved with Government and employers' associations, such as the Confederation of British Industry (C.B.I.), in discussions of national importance.

Types of union

It is not possible to categorise all unions in the United Kingdom into particular types, but a useful distinction may be made between:

2 Trade unions and their objectives

1. The craft union

Membership is restricted to individuals with a particular craft or skill irrespective of the industry in which they work. To join certain craft unions an individual must have completed his apprenticeship. Because certain skills are declining some craft unions have extended membership to include semi-skilled and unskilled workers, e.g. Amalgamated Union of Engineering Workers (A.U.E.W.).

2. The industrial union

Membership is restricted to employees within one industry irrespective of their occupation or grade. The National Union of Mineworkers (N.U.M.) and the National Union of Railwaymen (N.U.R.) are organised on industrial lines but both fail to cover the whole of their industry; the best examples of industrial unions occur in West Germany, which possesses 16 industrial unions.

3. The general union

Membership is not restricted to any particular industry or occupation and anybody may join. Two of the largest unions in the United Kingdom are 'general' unions. These are the Transport and General Workers' Union (T.G.W.U.) and The National Union of General and Municipal Workers (N.U.G.M.W.).

4. The white collar union

Membership is open to workers in non-manual employment; those working in offices as supervisors and technicians, etc. They may be organised around a single occupation, e.g. National Union of Teachers (N.U.T.) or the National Union of Bank Employees (N.U.B.E.), or they may cover a variety of occupations, e.g. Association of Scientific, Technical and Managerial Staffs (A.S.T.M.S.).

The aims of trade unions

Specific objectives

Although the aims vary between different unions they share four main objectives:

(a) To achieve improved conditions of employment for their members
Unions attempt to achieve this objective through negotiations for improved wages (see Table 1.1), shorter hours and longer holidays.

(b) To improve security of employment for their members
Unions have played a significant role in persuading the Government to

pass legislation giving workers greater job security. Under the Employment Protection Act (1975) an employee is entitled to one week's notice after four weeks' service and two weeks' notice after two years' service. The employee obtains an additional week's notice for each additional year of service, up to a maximum of twelve weeks. An employer planning redundancies must consult the appropriate union and take note of, and reply to, any representations made by them. A failure to consult the union can result in a 'protective award' which requires the employer to continue paying the employees affected by the redundancies for a specified period.

Table 1.1 Coal miners' improved wages, 1947–78

		Average weekly cash earnings (£)
Coal miners	1947	6.65
	1955	13.46
	1961	15.60
	1972	30.93
	1978	84.10

If an employer unfairly dismisses an employee (perhaps to avoid a redundancy payment) the latter, who is entitled to a written statement of the reasons for her dismissal, can complain to an industrial tribunal. It can, if the complaint is justified, reinstate the employee or award financial compensation.

The 1975 Act also provides protection for the pregnant woman. If she has been employed for at least two years and continues in employment until 11 weeks before the birth of her baby, the employer must pay her for the first 6 weeks of her absence. In addition, she can reclaim her job at any time up to 29 weeks after the birth.

Many trade unions have also negotiated comprehensive disciplinary procedures which entitle workers to formal verbal and written warnings before they may be dismissed, and which also give the right to have a trade union representative present when these warnings are given. Even when the formalities are complied with, the union may take collective action, such as a strike, to prevent the dismissal of a member or perhaps a reduction in earnings.

In these and many other ways union members are offered a considerable degree of security of employment and income.

(c) To improve the physical environment at work
Unions have striven for a more pleasant and safer environment within which their members work. They represent members injured at work, or suffering from diseases associated with the workplace, seeking maximum compensation from the employer.

Through safety and health legislation unions are increasingly monitoring safety and health standards at the workplace. Since 1 October 1978 they can appoint safety representatives whose main role is to monitor and inspect the workplace to identify and draw to management's attention any hazards which management may have overlooked.

(*d*) To offer members various monetary benefits
Although these benefits become less important with improved state benefits, most unions offer strike pay, sickness and death benefits to their members, or their next of kin.

These four **common** objectives relate to the individual member at her work place but trade unions possess other **general** and often longer-term objectives. In 1968 a Royal Commission investigated trade unions and employers' associations and the T.U.C. presented to the Commission seven further objectives.

General objectives

(*a*) *'Full employment' and national prosperity*
Unions increasingly involve themselves in matters of national concern. Since they believe every person should have the right to a job, they try to reduce unemployment by working with and through the Government and other bodies, such as the National Economic Development Council (N.E.D.C.). They seek higher levels of investment, the creation of new jobs and further-education schemes for unemployed school leavers in an attempt to reduce unemployment and improve national prosperity.

(*b*) *Improved social security schemes*
Unions have been active in trying to improve social security schemes to protect those unfortunate enough to be unemployed, sick or made redundant. Under the Redundancy Payments Act (1965) if a person's employment is terminated because her firm closes, or reduces its workforce, she receives a redundancy payment providing she has worked more than 16 hours per week for two years and is aged between 20 and 60 (65 if a man). The Act covers part-time staff who have worked for at least eight hours per week for the previous five years. The redundancy payment depends on the length of service but the maximum sum payable is £3,000.

(*c*) *Fair shares in national income and wealth*
Though unions have achieved improvements in wages and conditions of employment, they have failed to achieve a more equal distribution of income and wealth but this remains a long-term objective.

(d) Industrial democracy

Whilst most unions seek a greater involvement in the running of companies and organisations, there is little agreement between them how to achieve this. Some would like 'worker directors', appointed by trade union members, on the Board of Directors (a recommendation of the majority report of the 'Bullock Report on Industrial Democracy'); other unions are reluctant to become involved in the management of a company but prefer to extend collective bargaining as a mechanism for exercising control over management.

Legislation now recommends that companies should disclose any information to trade union representatives which makes collective bargaining more effective, such as financial information, manpower planning and investment plans. This should lead to a greater union involvement in the running of a company.

(e) A voice in Government

Trade unions are now consulted by Government on a wide range of issues, especially Government economic policy. On pay restraint the Government seeks the co-operation of the union movement and a realistic policy requires union approval. Unions have a considerable voice in Government and trade union critics argue that a Government is powerless in certain areas without the support of the union movement. The 'social contract' of the mid-1970s was an agreement between unions and Government. The former agreed to accept voluntary wage restraint in return for the Government's promise to restrict price rises, pass certain legislation (the Employment Protection Act) and create schemes to alleviate the worst effects of unemployment.

(f) Improved social and public services

Trade unions believe in strong social and public services (National Health, Social Services and Education) and voice their concern when public-spending cuts threaten their quality.

(g) Public control and planning of industry

Trade unions favour greater public control of industry through an extension of nationalisation. Even in the private sector they believe that Government and unions should be increasingly involved. The setting up of the National Enterprise Board (N.E.B.) reflects this objective.

Organisation of trade unions and employers' associations

Chapter 2

Trade unions

Sometimes employees possess the right to decide whether to become union members or not. However, if a **union membership agreement** (more commonly called the **closed shop**) exists it becomes a condition of employment that an employee *must* join the appropriate union (unless she is a member of specified religious sects which prohibit union membership).

1. Members

It is a **right** of any employee to join a trade union and her employer cannot victimise her because of it. If the employer refuses to recognise a trade union, the latter can ask A.C.A.S. (the Advisory, Conciliation and Arbitration Service) to investigate. If no amicable solution is found A.C.A.S. may recommend recognition. If the employer ignores this the union may complain to C.A.C. (the Central Arbitration Committee) who can make an enforceable award of terms and conditions of employment for the employees involved.

Once an individual decides to join a trade union she is obliged to comply with its rules and regularly pay her union dues. In return the union will negotiate on her behalf to improve her wages and working conditions. In addition they attempt to protect her against dismissal, change of job and take up any grievance with her employer. Finally, they provide her with services including legal advice, pensions advice and sick-pay schemes.

If a member fails to comply with the rules she may be fined, suspended, or, if in serious breach of the rules, dismissed from the union. If there is a closed shop this means effective dismissal from her employment.

2. Shop steward

Union members in a particular workplace elect a shop steward to act as
a representative on their behalf. If the workplace is large, a number of
shop stewards may be elected. They in turn may form themselves into a
joint shop stewards' committee which may consist of shop stewards
from several different unions. This committee elects a Chief Shop
Steward, often called a **convenor**, who acts as main spokesman for all
the unions.

Shop steward is the common title given to the representative elected
by the union members but she can also be known as **staff
representative**, **corresponding member** or (in the printing industry)
mother of the chapel.

The shop steward is an ordinary worker and is paid by the employer.
The amount of time spent on union activities varies from firm to firm.
Some employers help the shop steward perform her union duties by
providing facilities such as an office, telephone, clerical help and by
deducting union dues from the wage packets (the 'check off' system).

Being an elected representative, her main responsibility is to the
union members who elected her. She is also responsible for explaining
the union's policy to the membership which can sometimes create a
'conflict of loyalties'.

Her main duties are:

(*a*) recruitment of members;
(*b*) collecting union dues unless deducted at source by the firm;
(*c*) handling members' grievances;
(*d*) representing members' interests in discussions with management;
(*e*) developing trade union organisation at the workplace by achieving
    a good relationship with her own union hierarchy and liaising with
    other unions inside the workplace;
(*f*) keeping members informed of discussions with management and
    union policies;
(*g*) monitoring safety and health at the workplace.

3. The branch

When an employee joins a union she becomes a member of a **branch**.
This is the first level of the formal union organisation and is usually
based on the workplace or, if that is small, a geographical area. It holds
meetings on a regular basis, perhaps monthly, and all members are
entitled to attend, although attendance is generally very low. It is for
this reason that some organisations have always allowed branch
meetings to be held in worktime and now the Employment Protection
Act (1975) stipulates that employees shall be entitled to reasonable
time off in working hours to participate in union activities.

Branches are generally run on a voluntary, part-time basis by
members elected as Chairman, Branch Secretary and Treasurer

although some large branches are administered by a full-time official paid by the union.

The branch serves two functions. Firstly it administers **union affairs at local level**. This entails the formal admission of new members, the discussion and ratification of local agreements and the provision of a forum for the discussion of any matters of interest to the branch members. Its second function concerns **union affairs at a higher level**. It is the branch which elects delegates to **district** or **regional** committees (see below) and puts forward motions for discussion by these bodies. It is in these ways that branch members can become involved in the general running and policies of their union.

4. The district or region

Most unions group branches into **districts** or **regions** which provide the second formal level of union organisation. The branches elect delegates to the **district** or **regional committees** and these are generally assisted by full-time officials employed and paid by the union to implement district policy decisions. In some unions full-time officials working at **district** level stand for periodic re-election (even though paid employees of the union) but in other unions they are appointed to their posts.

The district committee monitors the running of the branches in their area and determines policy at **district** level, whilst their full-time officials may negotiate agreements with local firms and employers' associations. On rare occasions they may give official backing to industrial action though this is usually a national decision.

5. National Executive

Above the district committee is the **National Executive Committee** (sometimes **council**). This is composed of lay members elected on a regional basis (or by an **annual conference**) which in some unions is supplemented by full-time officials employed by the union. In exceptional cases it consists entirely of full-time officials.

The senior full-time official at national level is generally called the **general secretary** and is usually elected by members, holding the post until retiring age. He is the head of the union and controls all full-time officials as well as being **secretary** to the **National Executive Committee**. The general secretaries of six of the major unions are listed in Table 2.1.

The **National Executive Committee** is the most powerful permanent body in the union. It is responsible for administering the union and for putting into practice the policies adopted by the **annual conference**. It offers specialised facilities to its members, including education and training, and is the body which makes 'official' major strikes.

Table 2.1 Senior union officials

Union	General Secretary (1978)
N.U.M.	J. Gormley
T.G.W.U.	M. Evans
A.U.E.W.	T. Duffey
N.U.R.	S. Weighell
N.U.T.	F. Jarvis

6. The Conference or Congress

Most unions hold a yearly **conference** or **congress** where delegates, normally elected from **branches** or **districts** (in proportion to their membership), meet to determine the union's national policy.

The Executive Committee prepares a report on the previous year which is discussed by the delegates. Motions are submitted from branch, district and national level and resolutions passed which form the policy for the coming year. The conference is the supreme policy-making body of the union and exercises some control over the permanent **Executive Committee**. This body, in operating union affairs, is expected to consider the wishes of the union members as expressed democratically at the annual conference.

Trades Union Congress

Just as individual workers appreciated the benefits of combining together into trade unions, so the unions realised the importance of having one voice to speak for the trade union movement. In 1868 a permanent voluntary association of trade unions was founded which became known as the **Trades Union Congress** (T.U.C.). In 1977 the number of unions affiliated to the T.U.C. was 115 representing a total membership of 11,515,920. The T.U.C. determines and expresses unified policies for the trade union movement and works through Government to obtain implementation of these policies. To this end it is closely involved in issues of national importance to the movement, such as Government economic policy. Sometimes conflict develops between individual unions and the T.U.C. tries to avoid or to settle such disputes. It operates through three different bodies:

1. Annual Congress

Each affiliated union sends 1 delegate per 5,000 members to the Annual Congress. This body reviews the work of the General Council of the previous year, discusses and determines broad policy and elects the General Council for the coming year.

2. General Council

This consists of the General Secretary and Assistant General Secretary of the T.U.C. with the other members elected by the Annual Congress. Most of the work is performed by committees such as the 'Economic Committee' and the 'Collective Bargaining Committee' which translate the broad policy determined at Congress into practical policy decisions. This is then reviewed by the Council at their regular meetings.

The T.U.C. also acts as a peacemaker, intervening in industrial disputes (if requested by the unions involved) and investigating inter-union disputes with the contestants' consent. Its members sit on numerous national bodies including the N.E.D.C. as well as conducting discussions with the C.B.I. and the Government.

3. General Secretary and full-time staff

The General Secretary controls the full-time staff and as chief spokesman for the trade-union movement is prominent in the mass media. He exercises considerable influence but is bound by the wishes of the General Council. The full-time staff are organised into six main departments:

(*a*) economic;
(*b*) production;
(*c*) social insurance;
(*d*) international;
(*e*) organisation;
(*f*) education;

and their main functions are to:

(i) conduct detailed research and provide the various committees with information;
(ii) offer advice and information to member unions;
(iii) organise training of trade union representatives at Congress House (T.U.C. headquarters) and in the regions through Trade Union Centres and Further Education Colleges;
(iv) run local organisations (Trades Councils) which the T.U.C. uses to disseminate information

Employers' associations

Just as employees with a common interest formed trade unions, so employers with a common trade or industrial interest joined together to form employers' associations. These can be organised nationally with regional branches but they usually consist of local associations, representing local employers, affiliated to a national federation. There are 35 district engineering employers' associations affiliated to the engineering employers' federation.

Local associations elect representatives to the national council who supervise the federation's paid officials (the management board) headed by the director. In practice the director and senior officials in conjunction with a few major employers make most major decisions.

Employers' associations' functions are to:

(*a*) assist with industrial relations. This includes representing members in negotiations with unions or before industrial tribunals and advising on industrial issues;

(*b*) advise on trade, technical and commercial matters such as research into technical progress, standard forms of contracts, etc.;

(*c*) assist with education and training, many associations providing training courses on safety and health and supervisory management specifically related to their members' needs;

(*d*) represent employers' views to government and other bodies, often via the Confederation of British Industry (see below).

Any firm can join the appropriate employers' association but a failure to abide by federation decisions can lead to reprimand or expulsion. Large employers wishing to manage their affairs independently, not being bound by national agreements, and small firms desirous of retaining their flexibility often remain outside their national associations.

Confederation of British Industry

This was formed in 1965 and consists of 12,500 firms, 250 employers' associations, the nationalised industries and some commercial undertakings. It is the employers' counterpart of the T.U.C., acting as industry's spokesman, seeking to consult, advise and influence the Government. It has close liaison with the T.U.C. on matters of common interest (unemployment, pay, etc.), often sitting on the same committees (N.E.D.C.).

Examination questions

1.
Trades Union Congress
|
Executive Committees
|
District Committees
|
Branches
|
Shop stewards
|
Members

12 Organisation of trade unions and employers' associations

(a) Briefly explain this simplified diagram of trade union organisation.
(b) Explain the essential differences between the following types of unions:
  (i) Craft union
  (ii) Industrial union
  (iii) White collar unions
  (iv) General unions

(Q. 10   1977)

2. What are the main functions of shop stewards?

(Q. 3   1975)

3. A newspaper article commented that 'white-collar workers will exercise greater economic strength in the future'. Who are the white-collar workers?

(Q. 1(c)   1974)

Sample questions

1. Give examples of the types of issue that might involve the Government consulting the C.B.I. and the T.U.C.

2. What do you understand by the term 'union membership agreement', more commonly known as the 'closed shop'?

3. Name two trade unions with which you are familiar and explain the types of workers who become members.

4. Write an imaginary news report on 'a day in the life of a trade union General Secretary'. The report should bring out his involvement with his members, the employers and the Government.

Collective bargaining
Chapter 3

Most of the working population have their wages and other conditions of service determined by collective bargaining between their trade unions and their employers or the employers' association, although increasingly the Government is laying down guidelines within which the negotiations must be conducted.

Negotiations can be at two levels, local and national, both of which are described below.

Local negotiations

These involve bargaining between shop stewards and plant management. This form of negotiation grew in the 1960s with the development of incentive schemes and productivity deals. There is little involvement with paid union officials, who only intervene where the issues are important or negotiations break down. Although providing flexibility, local bargaining possesses serious disadvantages which have been particularly noticeable in the car industry. Where workers, perhaps fitters, in one plant negotiate a favourable overtime rate, employees in a different plant will claim parity with this group thereby producing escalating wages. In a plant with different unions, if one negotiates better fringe benefits than the other, the latter will immediately claim parity with similar results. Because of these defects most companies are attempting to replace local bargaining by nationally agreed conditions of service.

Basic wage rates are determined nationally but since bonus rates, piece rates, etc. may be fixed locally, this allows shop stewards to negotiate significant monetary benefits for their members. Other matters previously negotiated locally have become the subject of national agreements or legislation. The establishment of the closed shop was often negotiated locally but this is now usually a company-wide decision, as in British Rail.

Most local agreements are written but some are oral, often having been established through custom and practice. Despite their origins these are as rigorously enforced as written agreements.

National

These involve negotiations between the employers' association and the union. They may meet on an *ad hoc* basis or more formally, with perhaps the establishment of a standing national joint industrial council. In most areas collective bargaining developed on a voluntary *ad hoc* basis but a statutory requirement exists in nationalised industries to establish a collective bargaining mechanism and where an industry is weakly organised on the union side the Government establishes a minimum wage-fixing authority (wages council).

Agreements negotiated nationally cover main principles, thereby allowing member firms flexibility in their implementation. They usually encompass minimum rates of pay, length of working week, holiday entitlements and overtime payments, although other issues may be dealt with.

Collective bargaining involves negotiating and sometimes the parties may be unable to agree. This has led to the development of disputes procedures. Assuming the dispute is at local level a **works conference** is called involving full-time union officials and representatives from the local employers' associations. If the dispute is not resolved a **local conference** is called involving the district organisations. Finally a **national conference** is called involving the union executive and senior officials of the employers' association. The parties may use the services of the Advisory Conciliation and Arbitration Council (A.C.A.S.) whose function is to persuade them to consider every possible solution (they act as conciliators). A.C.A.S. do not recommend solutions, although if requested they can arrange an arbitration. They do not arbitrate but provide an acceptable arbitrator or arbitrators, who, having listened to the evidence, will propose a solution. Although not usually legally binding there is a moral obligation for the parties to accept.

Where collective bargaining fails to resolve a dispute the union may take industrial action. This could involve a strike (withdrawal of labour), random wildcat strikes seeking to disrupt the industry, a factory occupation, a go-slow or work-to-rule (which involves sticking rigidly to job descriptions and the formal conditions of employment).

Free collective bargaining

The term 'free collective bargaining' means that the parties to a dispute can resolve it without interference from a third party. Free collective bargaining has been undermined by Government intervention through:

1. The establishment of wages councils to set minimum wages in industries lacking strong unions, such as retailing and catering.
2. The passing of legislation. The Contracts of Employment Act (as amended by the Employment Protection Act) requires employers to provide employees with written conditions of employment containing specified information. Even in 1946 the Fair Wages Resolution impelled employers involved in government contract work to pay their employees a set rate. The Government establishes legal minimum standards below which an employer cannot negotiate. The most well-known intervention is through 'wages and incomes policies' where the Government fixes an upper limit on wage increases.
3. Direct Government intervention in the dispute. This is usually necessary to safeguard the health, safety or security of the nation. In the late 1970s the British Fire Service went on strike for more pay and the Army manned the fire stations because of the threat to life.

Joint consultation

This involves a *discussion* of common problems between employers and employees (as occurs in the N.E.D.C.) and must be distinguished from collective bargaining, which entails *negotiating*. Many issues previously the province of joint consultation have now moved into the collective-bargaining sphere. Years of pay restraint have increased union interest in fringe benefits (pensions, canteen facilities and welfare) previously discussed in joint consultation. The growth of health and safety legislation has also removed subjects which were historically very important, thereby minimising further the role of joint consultation.

Examination questions

1. Give **two** examples of issues which might be the subject of 'collective bargaining'.
   (Q. 1(j)   1977)

2. What is the meaning of the terms:
   (*a*) conciliation
   (*b*) arbitration?
   (Q. 1(f)   1975)

Sample questions

1. Give **three** examples of ways in which the Government intervenes in the 'free collective bargaining' process.
2. Distinguish between 'joint consultation' and 'collective bargaining'.

Training
Chapter 4

The effectiveness of any organisation depends on the quality of its staff and the training they receive. This is an ongoing process commencing with the induction of new employees followed by further training, on or off the job, varying from a few days to several years.

Training serves three basic needs.

1. To provide new employees with the necessary skills and knowledge to enable them to perform their new jobs and settle into their new work environment.
2. To prepare existing employees for changes in their jobs. These may arise from the introduction of new processes, materials or new products. Training will also be necessary to enable promoted staff to cope with their new responsibilities.
3. To improve efficiency within a specified area. Large retail groups run periodic training sessions aimed at reducing shoplifting. Factories run courses in safety to reduce the number of accidents and all organisations hold management courses to improve the efficiency of their senior staff.

Types of training

1. Induction

Most employers have recognised the value of induction training in making new workers productive more quickly. Sally Smith has recently left a further education college to start employment and details of her induction programme are given in Fig. 4.1.

This illustrates three main features of induction courses.

(a) The *personal* part of the programme introduces the new employee to her colleagues and shows her where she will be working. She is

Fig. 4.1 Induction programme for Sally Smith

First half day	Report to main Personnel Office

Terms of employment Explanation of:
 (i) Hours of work
 (ii) Holiday entitlement
 (iii) Sickness provision
 (iv) Notice periods
 (v) Absence – permission
 (vi) Pay arrangements
 (vii) Pension schemes
 (viii) Contract of Employment
Coffee

Safety and health Explanation of:
 (i) Safety precautions
 (ii) Fire drill and alarms
 (iii) Medical services and first aid

Facilities Explanation of, and tour (where relevant):
 (i) Canteens
 (ii) Personnel Dept.
 (iii) Welfare arrangements
 (iv) Sports and Social club
 (v) Savings schemes

Introduction to workplace
 (i) Introduction to immediate colleagues
 (ii) Tour of work area
 (iii) Toilet and other facilities

Lunch with new colleagues

Afternoon Return to Personnel Office

The Company
Introduction to Company by senior member of Management.
Products and future plans of Company.
Film of history and development of the Company.

Guided tour of Company

Tea

Industrial relations Explanation of:
 (i) Trade unions in Company
 (ii) Right to join
 (iii) Joint consultative machinery
 (iv) Grievance procedure
 (v) Introduction to local shop steward

INDUCTION PROGRAMME (continued)

Second day	Report to immediate supervisor
	Job familiarisation Explanation of work to be done. Demonstration of various equipment to be used. Practice
	Coffee
	Meeting with Personnel Officer
	Allocation to experienced employee in section for rest of 1st week.

informed of company policy on pay, clocking in, job documentation, safety precautions, fire drills, etc. She is also given a tour and shown the canteen, toilets and sports facilities. Finally she is introduced to the Personnel Department who can answer any queries arising during her first days at work.

(*b*) The second part of the programme provides the new employee with *an overall picture of the company*. She is told their history, their main markets, the products they manufacture and she may be given a tour of the whole company in order to appreciate her section's role within the organisation.

(*c*) The third part aims at *familiarising the new employee with her job* by giving her a demonstration followed by practise in a simulated work environment. The induction programme will be supported by practical training on the job.

2. Technical and commercial

Most organisations requiring skilled workers possess apprenticeship or training programmes lasting several years. These consist of working within the company, supported by off-the-job training on day-release or block-release basis. This type of training enables the employee to acquire both theoretical and practical knowledge. In some large organisations apprentices or trainees work in different departments to broaden their work experience.

3. Supervisory and managerial

In the past, staff were often promoted from the shop floor to supervisory or managerial positions without training. Most organisations today would regard this as unacceptable. The skills required by the shop-floor worker and the supervisor or manager are totally different, the former having no experience of giving orders, report writing, negotiating with trade unions and dealing with

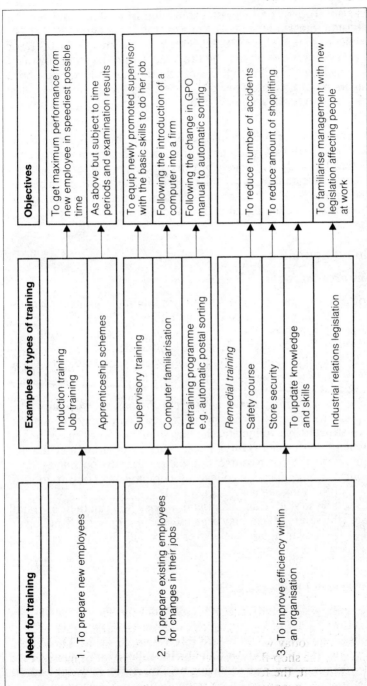

Need for training	Examples of types of training	Objectives
1. To prepare new employees	Induction training Job training	To get maximum performance from new employee in speediest possible time
	Apprenticeship schemes	As above but subject to time periods and examination results
2. To prepare existing employees for changes in their jobs	Supervisory training	To equip newly promoted supervisor with the basic skills to do her job
	Computer familiarisation	Following the introduction of a computer into a firm
	Retraining programme e.g. automatic postal sorting	Following the change in GPO manual to automatic sorting
3. To improve efficiency within an organisation	*Remedial training* Safety course	To reduce number of accidents
	Store security	To reduce amount of shoplifting
	To update knowledge and skills	
	Industrial relations legislation	To familiarise management with new legislation affecting people at work

Fig. 4.2   Need for training and types of training

grievances. To assist a successful transition from shop floor to supervision, most companies organise a training programme in basic principles of supervision and management. These are usually of one or two weeks' duration and may be provided within the company or by outside agencies (see below). Even fully trained and experienced managers require courses to update their knowledge and these are offered by universities, schools of business management and private bodies.

The above are the three main types of training, but mention must be made of short courses which are a prominent feature of the training scene (see Fig. 4.2). These may be remedial (an organisation having a high level of accidents may organise a series of short courses on health and safety at work), but the majority of short courses are run to update staff on recent technological and legal changes.

Training agencies

1. The organisation

Almost every organisation performs some internal training (induction training can only be effectively done within the firm). On-the-job training is given to employees in the normal working situation, the employee being regarded as a partly productive worker until she reaches a certain standard, and may involve a new employee being assigned to an experienced employee who shows her what to do ('sitting next to Nellie').

Off-the-job training occurs away from the normal working environment. An employee is not regarded as a productive worker. She is instructed by a trained teacher in a simulated work environment and when fully trained returns to the working environment. Large employers run their own courses but smaller firms use outside agencies including further education colleges. A comparison of on-the-job and off-the-job training is given in Table 4.1.

In addition to skills training, organisations often run their own staff courses (the safety officer may organise a course on safer handling of goods). The advantage of these over externally organised courses is one of cost and convenience.

2. Colleges of further education

These offer full- and part-time courses, ranging from professional and secretarial to apprenticeship schemes. Many are designed to satisfy a local need and have developed as a result of liaison with local industries. The growth of management departments in the colleges was a direct result of the growing demand for management and supervisory courses.

Table 4.1

Advantages	Disadvantages
On-the-job	
1. It is cheaper as existing staff and equipment can be utilised. 2. The learning is done in a more realistic environment, removing the need for the student to readjust from a learning to a work environment.	1. The employee to whom the new employee is attached may be a poor teacher and be unable to teach the proper skills. 2. If the employee has developed bad habits these will be transferred to the new employee. 3. The work situation may be noisy and stressful, not the best learning conditions.
Off-the-job	
1. Because teaching is performed in a training environment it can be planned, with the student acquiring knowledge in stages. This may allow her to become productive more quickly. 2. The trained instructor will ensure that new employees are taught the best methods. 3. Training is conducted in a less stressful situation. 4. Being under constant supervision there is less chance of damaging machinery, etc.	1. It may be expensive (e.g. setting up workshops, cost of accommodation, etc.). 2. Students may find readjustment from the training to the work situation difficult.

In addition to their normal work, colleges liaise with the Training Services Division (T.S.D.) to provide courses for unemployed school leavers and those wishing to retrain under the training opportunities scheme (see Table 4.2).

Table 4.2 Training Opportunities Scheme

	Total TOPS trainees	% in skill centres	% in F.E.
1971	15,600	82	NIL
1978	77,000	26	62

3. Specialist centres

Many organisations provide specialist courses for their members; these include The Institute of Personnel Management and the Industrial Society. Courses organised by employers' associations, for example The Engineering Employers' Association, for their

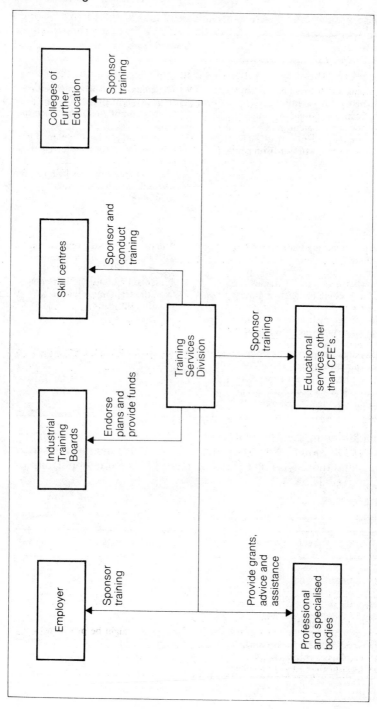

Fig. 4.3 Main agencies for training and their link with the training services division

confederation members are especially useful for smaller firms unable to run specialised courses.

(a) *Industrial training boards*
These were established by the Government to implement the 1964 Industrial Training Act. They cover a wide range of activities such as agriculture, hotel and catering, engineering and retail distribution, and consist of an independent chairman, representatives from employers and employees and the educational service. Their function is to ensure that adequate training exists within their industry. They run courses, support colleges and other establishments, research into particular problems and publish information on training. The training boards are co-ordinated and mainly financed by the Manpower Services Agency.

(b) *Training Services Division*
The Training Services Division (T.S.D.), a branch of the Manpower Services Agency, is responsible for organising and running courses under the Training Opportunities Scheme (TOPS). This aims at retraining men and women wishing to change their occupations or recommence work after a period of inactivity. See Fig. 4.3.

Examination questions

1. Many organisations give employees induction training. What do you consider to be the main aspects that should be covered in an induction programme?
(Q. 12   1977)

2. Explain with an example the difference between 'on-the-job training' and 'off-the-job training'.
(Q. 1(k)   1975)

3. Give **three** examples of training which take place in industry and discuss the ways in which they might be expected to make industry more efficient.
(Q. 2   1975)

Sample questions

1. A medium-sized company has drawn up a training programme for the coming year which includes:
   (a) induction training;
   (b) safety training;
   (c) apprentice training;
   (d) management and supervisory training;
   (e) administrative and clerical training.
   Select any **three** of these forms of training and explain the need and benefits to be derived from such training.

2. Give examples of the types of training provision which might be provided by the following agencies for training:
   (a) employees own company;
   (b) local further education college;
   (c) training board

3. Explain the abbreviation 'TOPS'.

Communications in business

Chapter 5

Good communications and good morale are usually linked, and a breakdown in communications has been responsible for many recent industrial disputes, with the subsequent loss of production. A good communications system is therefore essential to the efficiency, and possibly the survival, of a firm. It should be one of the first priorities of management: as Chester Barnard said, 'The first executive function is to develop and maintain a system of communications.'

To understand the connection between communication and morale one must distinguish between one-way and two-way communication. The former makes no provision for any reaction or response from the receiver of the information. Two-way communication involves a response. A directive on a noticeboard is a one-way communication whereas an interview or an efficient suggestions scheme involves two-way communication.

Good communications systems do not arise haphazardly but require planning. In most organisations the formal channels of communication can be found by examining the organisation structure. There is a direct relationship between lines of authority and communication channels and Fig. 5.1 indicates the lines of authority and communication within one organisation. The Managing Director links his Board of Directors and the management team and is responsible for passing information between the two. Figure 5.1 also indicates that the foreman is the communications link between the workforce and the superintendent. The line organisation shows that, in theory, a communications link exists between the Managing Director and the workforce.

A foreman with a personnel problem, using these channels of communication, would need to go via the Managing Director and the Personnel Manager to obtain advice from the personnel department. Such a system would be cumbersome and unworkable, therefore in most organisations there is a formal system of lateral communications (i.e. horizontal as opposed to vertical). Problems can arise if the

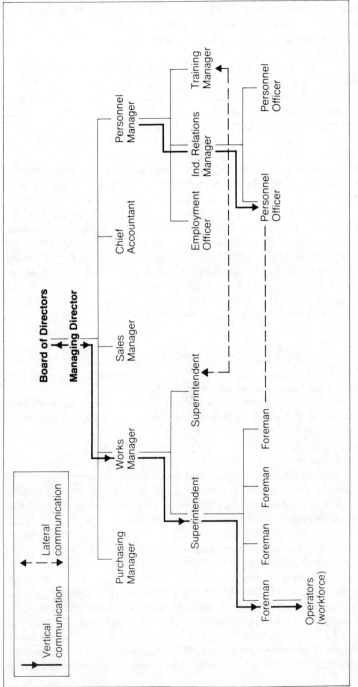

Fig. 5.1

foreman and the Personnel Officer solve their problem without informing their superiors, and to avoid this interdepartmental committees or memos are used as an integral part of lateral communications.

Merely possessing an organisation chart does not guarantee good communications. People within the organisation must know what their functions are. Where management inadequately defines authority and responsibility, employees may be confused about their particular role within the communications process. This leads to overlap or omission. It is therefore essential that job descriptions exist which define responsibilities and duties with regard to communications.

Formal communications channels often break down when they consist of too many levels. By increasing the numbers through whom a communication must pass, the possibilities of distortion are increased and whilst this may be minimised by using written communications, the possibilities of a message not being passed on still remain. A method of overcoming this might be joint consultation with the members representing different levels within the organisation. The proliferation of management layers is usually associated with the size of firm. Another problem of size is the possible isolation of employees from central management. To reduce the likelihood that the large number of memos and notices sent from Head Office will be disregarded, it may be necessary to decentralise, giving authority to individual plants or branches.

In addition to formal communications channels, all organisations possess informal channels, although these are more active where formal communications are inadequate. Some informal channels are highly developed and extremely efficient, often being quicker than more formalised ones. The former all possess an inherent defect because management cannot control the input of information and actions may be taken without their knowledge.

Informal channels may develop because of friendships within the organisation. Friends may telephone each other to gossip or speed up their work by circumventing a bureaucratic communications system. The most common method of informal communication is the casual conversation between employees, often called the 'grapevine'. This usually works against the organisation's interests by spreading rumour and creating unnecessary worries. An effective management should therefore eliminate the grapevine by keeping all workers informed, especially supervisory management so they can help allay any fears arising on the shop floor. Whilst the grapevine needs cutting down, other informal methods may be incorporated into the formal structure. Informal channels often grow because of the formal structure's defects and their incorporation will improve the latter. Where an informal system of lateral communications has developed it may be formalised by interdepartmental meetings. There is, however, a danger of making the communications structure too formal. Where the formal structure is strictly adhered to and informal communications are discouraged this may stop two individuals communicating to solve a problem, thereby causing inefficiency and frustration amongst the individuals concerned.

Methods of communication

1. Written

As well as letters to employees, interdepartmental memos, etc. these include:

(a) *House journals and magazines*
These contain information about the firm's business and social activities, on the theory that as employees read the latter they will notice the business news. This enables the firm to disseminate information on current performance and future plans. Assessing their effectiveness is difficult but they do provide a mechanism for disseminating information in larger organisations.

(b) *Notice boards*
These are effective providing certain basic rules are observed. They must be strategically positioned in accessible places, strict control must be exercised over material posted on them, they should be kept neat and tidy and outdated notices removed.

Written communications are less ambiguous and less open to misinterpretation than oral communications and they also provide a permanent record. They are, however, impersonal, do not allow questions and there is no guarantee that the recipient reads the communication.

2. Tannoy systems

These possess a limited use, having the disadvantages of written communications without the advantages.

3. Large meetings

Some organisations hold meetings to inform staff about important issues. Where the organisation is large these will be held at branch or department level. To obtain maximum benefit from such meetings they must be well structured with the opportunity for questions, although as employees often feel inhibited from asking questions they are usually one-way.

4. Small committees

The advantage of these is that they enable a two-way flow of information and may improve lateral communications. Those attending such meetings must inform their subordinates of committee decisions.

5. Personal meetings or interviews

These allow a two-way flow of information and the person issuing instructions can ask questions to ensure she has been fully understood.

6. Joint consultation (i.e. a committee of employers and employees)

The authoritative nature of many old managements resulted in a breakdown in two-way communications and an isolation of the workforce. To improve the situation modern management has attempted to involve workers in management through joint consultation. Monthly meetings, held during working hours, consider matters of general interest such as training and canteen facilities. Matters which are the subject of negotiation or dispute, such as pay and conditions of service, are excluded. Latest evidence suggests that joint consultation as a mechanism for improving communications is losing popularity as many issues discussed are regarded by employees as trivial. Trade unionists have therefore preferred to concentrate their energies in improving bargaining power at plant level. The future of joint consultation depends on whether important issues are discussed and whether management will take union suggestions seriously.

Methods 4–6 provide two-way communication allowing the speaker to detect the mood, attitude and response of the other party. However, these forms of communication, especially where large numbers are involved, can lead to inaccuracy and misunderstanding. Verbal communications must therefore be supported by minutes or memorandums which are less open to misinterpretation and provide a permanent record.

7. Joint activity (industrial democracy)

The decline of joint consultation has coincided with the increasing power of the local trade unionist and it has been argued that the logical extension of joint consultation is industrial democracy. This means employers and employees join together not merely to consult but to make decisions. The Bullock Report (1977) proposed a programme which, if implemented, would have meant worker-directors on the boards of major companies. The majority report was rejected by British management and not implemented. If, however, the UK is to adopt EEC practices, some form of worker participation in the decision-making process seems inevitable.

Foreign experience of industrial democracy

1. Sweden

The Swedish worker-director system was introduced in 1973 and provides two worker seats on single-tier company boards which traditionally have between six and eight directors. In addition two further reserve worker-directors sit in on meetings and join in discussions but they cannot vote. It may be argued that such an arrangement allows worker-directors to gather information and influence decisions rather than share in power. It is also common for the worker-directors to leave the boardroom when industrial action or wage bargaining is discussed, which emphasises the importance still placed on collective bargaining.

2. Germany

Germany operates a two-tier system, i.e. a supervisory board below the main board. Employees' representatives have half the seats on the supervisory board but they include one nominee from senior management and the chairman possesses the casting vote in a situation of deadlock. This in reality gives the shareholders a built-in majority.

Although many of the employee representatives are union members the system is not union based and is open to all employees. The power of the German supervisory boards is overshadowed by that wielded by all-employee works councils which, as well as wide-ranging powers of access to information, have rights of co-determination with employers on issues relating to manpower. Because of this, employee representatives on boards have only had limited impact.

Because of the different traditional cultures, legal systems, and the different climate of industrial relations it is difficult to see how the foreign experience of industrial participation can be transferred to British industry without considerable qualification and modifications.

Defective communications

Many reasons exist for unsatisfactory communications.

1. Lack of policy

Unless management possess a coherent policy, effective communications are impossible.

2. Use of wrong media

Many methods of communicating are one-way, not allowing any response from employees. These are suitable for giving simple instructions but inappropriate where delicate issues of company policy are involved. The use of the wrong media to communicate information can result in unanswered questions, which lead to gossip and distortions of the truth. A letter in employees' pay packets stating that a large export order has been cancelled may instigate rumours of redundancy because of lack of work. If this information is presented at a meeting an employees' representative may raise the question of possible redundancies, thereby giving management the opportunity to allay any unjustified fears.

3. Inability of the communicators

A communications system is only as good as those who operate it. 'Personnel' problems which hamper good communications include:

(a) Fixed attitudes
Where management is authoritarian and old fashioned, communications are often one-way with little feedback from the employees. The latter become frustrated and isolated from management which may cause a 'them and us' attitude. Management and unions become enemies rather than partners which makes fruitful communication more difficult.

(b) Past record
If the firm's past record is poor this will inhibit progress towards implementing a more effective system. The employees may view management communications with suspicion, resulting in the development of the hostile grapevine.

(c) Inability to respond
Management is now required by both unions and legislation to communicate far more information to the employee. This poses problems as the latter often lack the expertise to understand this information. The average shop-floor worker finds balance sheets, profit-and-loss accounts and manpower planning difficult to understand. The unions appreciate this and now run specialised courses to help their representatives understand the information they are entitled to receive.

(d) Power groups
Every organisation harbours numerous power groups. These may be union versus management but often such groupings exist within union or management. A firm's employees may be represented by several unions, each seeking to establish itself as the dominant union. Within management, departments may be attempting to strengthen their position within the organisation by claiming an increased share of the organisation's resources. In these circumstances communications may be distorted because the groups use the communications process for

their own advantage. One of management's tasks is therefore to remove these rivalries so communications can flow unhindered.

Individuals will use the communications network more effectively if they possess training in:

1. Communications skills

Certain technical communications skills can be improved by training and planned experience. This might involve courses in more effective use of meetings, report writing, interviewing skills and presentation of data.

2. Human relations

Effective communications means presenting information in the correct manner. This involves management appreciating the impact the information will have on the recipient. A manager must realise that a much-needed reorganisation can be viewed by the shop floor as yet another threat to their jobs. If the real fears of workers are understood the case for reorganisation can be expressed in a way that allays these fears. A failure to appreciate the fears, prejudices and perhaps hostility of the workforce has caused many of the current industrial problems. The effective channels of communication have served not to improve industrial relations but to worsen them.

Note of caution

Too much communication is as dangerous as too little. Overcommunication, in its worst form, means that individuals are so involved with committees, reports, memos and other forms of paperwork that these become an end in themselves. Every organisation should question the value of every communication and should abolish any that are unnecessary. In 1956 Marks and Spencer eliminated 26 million pieces of paper per annum to reduce the paperwork within their organisation, thereby helping to improve effective communication.

Examination questions

1. The larger the organisation the more difficult effective communications become. Why should this be so? What steps might be taken to minimise the risk of ineffective communications in the large organisation?

   (Q. 9 1977)

2. We often read in newspapers about 'breakdown of communications between management and workers'. What methods might be employed to improve such communications?

   (Q. 9 1976)

3. Explain the term 'joint consultation'. How might its use be expected to promote better communications in industry?

(Q. 4   1975)

4. Discuss some of the methods the management of a firm can use to communicate with their workers.

(Q. 2   1974)

Sample questions

1. Explain the ways in which 'organisation charts' and 'job descriptions' help effective communications within a business.

2. Distinguish between 'formal' and 'informal' communications. Identify some of the ways in which informal communications can benefit an organisation.

3. Discuss some of the main difficulties of making communications within an organisation effective.

4. The noticeboard provides the employer with a cheap, efficient method of communicating with all employees.
   (a) What reservations would you list about the use of the noticeboard as a main means of communicating with large numbers of employees?
   (b) Draw up a simple list of rules which you would apply to obtain the maximum benefit from the use of a noticeboard.

Business organisations
Chapter 6

Private sector

In this sector an organisation's major objective is profit maximisation with little emphasis on social and economic objectives.

1. Sole trader

This is the simplest type of business to start (or finish), involving few legal formalities and limited capital. Many successful companies started as sole traders: Unilever originated from William Lever's Bolton grocery business and Marks and Spencer from the penny bazaar. The sole trader owns her own business, usually makes all the decisions (even though she may employ staff), receives all the profits and bears all the losses. It is the most common business organisation but relatively insignificant as an employer. Sole traders are common amongst specialist retailers, service trades (hairdressers, plumbers, window cleaners, etc.) and professions (accountants, architects, etc.)

Such businesses possess two main disadvantages. Firstly, they have unlimited liability. This means business creditors can claim business and personal assets in settlement of debts. Secondly, they are unable to raise large sums of capital. This is usually the owner's (or her relatives' or friends') savings, and although profits may be retained this is a slow method of raising finance. For this reason, expanding sole traders often consider other forms of business organisation. The advantages and disadvantages are listed in Table 6.1.

2. Partnerships

These are groups of more than two people carrying on a business with a view to making a profit. A sole trader might choose partnership to increase her business capital and widen the breadth and scope of

Table 6.1 Advantages and disadvantages of the sole trader

Advantages	Disadvantages
1. Offers a personal service. 2. Better relationship with employees, hence higher staff morale. 3. More flexible, quicker response to changes in demand. 4. Can produce products where limited demand. 5. Greater management control. 6. Can cater for a local need. 7. Being one's own boss. 8. Receives all profits, therefore strong incentive towards efficiency.	1. Inability to raise large sums of capital. 2. Unlimited liability. 3. Unable to obtain economies of scale. 4. More vulnerable to economic recessions. 5. Taxation problems on owner's death. 6. Growth of paperwork necessary to run a small business. 7. Unable to conduct research and development. 8. Lack of continuity of management on death.

management, each partner often specialising in one aspect of the business. The maximum number of partners is 20 (10 in banking) except for accountants, solicitors, stockbrokers and jobbers where there is no limit.

In ordinary partnerships each partner usually provides part of the capital and profits are shared as agreed in the Deed of Partnership. Each active partner is involved in management and all her decisions (even if unauthorised) bind the other partners. Whilst **active partners** are involved in management and share the profits and losses, **sleeping**

Table 6.2 Advantages and disadvantages of partnerships

Advantages	Disadvantages
Ordinary	
1. Greater management expertise than sole trader. 2. Greater capital available than with sole trader. 3. Retains personal contact lost in large organisations. 4. Provides greater continuity of management than with a sole trader.	1. All partners can bind the firm. 2. Limit to capital that can be raised. 3. Automatic dissolution of partnership on death or bankruptcy of any partner. 4. Unlimited liability. 5. The consent of all partners is required before a new partner can be admitted.
Limited	
1. Limited liability. 2. Receives share of profits although not actively involved in management.	1. Cannot withdraw her capital without the consent of the other partner. 2. No share in management.

partners play no part in management although they share profits and losses. As with sole traders the partners possess unlimited liability.

The Limited Partnership Act permits partners with limited liability (**limited partners**) providing they are not involved in the firm's management *and* one partner possess unlimited liability. A retired partner acting in an advisory capacity could be a limited partner. Limited partnerships require registering with the Registrar of Joint-Stock Companies.

Partnerships are uncommon in the manufacturing sector and are usually found in the professions (solicitors, dentists, doctors, architects, etc.), where business risks are minimal and where the professional bodies often forbid their members forming companies. Where the partnership name differs from that of the partners it must be registered under the Registration of Business Names Act. Once registration is complete a certificate is issued which permits trading under the assumed name. The advantages and disadvantages are listed in Table 6.2. Where possible, partnerships usually seek company status to acquire limited liability.

3. Joint-stock companies

There are three types of companies:

Chartered
These are created by Royal Charter (for example the Bank of England). The granting of new charters is rare and mainly confined to professional organisations.

Statutory
These are formed by special Acts of Parliament, examples being British Rail and the National Coal Board.

Registered
These can be:

(i) *Unlimited.* These are rare as they do not confer limited liability.

(ii) *Limited by guarantee.* These are common in non-trading enterprises (for example examining boards). The company members guarantee a fixed sum if liquidation occurs and profits are usually used to further the organisation's aims.

(iii) *Limited by shares.* These can be private or public companies. **Private companies** consist of between 2 and 50 shareholders, exclusive of employees who hold shares. The shareholders possess limited liability (hence its advantage over partnership), but the company cannot raise capital by a public issue and shares cannot be transferred without all the shareholders' approval. Because of their limited size the owners are often involved in management and this type of organisation is usually limited to medium-size commercial or industrial organisations (often family firms). They outnumber public companies but are smaller and less important as employers and producers.

Public companies require at least seven shareholders but there is no maximum. The shares can be offered to the public, are freely transferable on the Stock Exchange and the shareholders possess limited liability. The company possesses a legal identity distinct from its shareholders, hence a shareholder's death does not effect the company's existence (compare with partnership). With numerous shareholders the firm's management and ownership is divorced. The shareholders (owners) elect a board of directors to run the company and although they have to verbally present an annual report at the Annual General Meeting when they are accountable for their year of stewardship, they possess considerable freedom. As with private companies they must send their audited accounts to the Registrar of Companies each year.

To form a registered company two documents must be filed with the Registrar of Joint-Stock Companies. The *Memorandum of Association* defines the company's constitution and powers, indicating its relationship with the outside world (the 'external rules'). It includes the name of the company (with 'limited' as the last word), a detailed statement of its objects, the amount of the share capital with the nominal value of each share, a declaration of association signed by seven shareholders (two with a private company) and the address of the registered office. The *Articles of Association* are the rules governing the management of the company (its internal affairs). It covers the issue of shares, their transfer, conduct of general meetings, voting rights and the powers and duties of directors.

A public company must also file a list of directors with the written consent of each attached. On receipt of the above documents the Registrar issues a certificate of incorporation, and where necessary a trading certificate, permitting the company to commence business.

A company's *authorised* (or *nominal*) capital need not all be immediately issued to shareholders. The amount allocated to them is the *issued* capital. The *called-up capital* is the amount paid for each issued share, which may be less than its face value.

Nominal capital   2,500,000 × £1 shares
Issued capital   1,500,000
Called-up   50p per share
Capital received by company   50p × 1,500,000 = £750,000
Additional capital is available by calling up 50p from existing shareholders and issuing the other 1,000,000 shares.

Once incorporated, a company has 'perpetual succession'; it continues until it fails to make an annual return, becomes insolvent or the shareholders request its liquidation. The advantages and disadvantages of companies are listed in Table 6.3.

Table 6.3 Advantages and disadvantages of companies

Advantages	Disadvantages
1. Large sums of capital can be raised. 2. Shareholders possess limited liability. 3. Continuity of management. 4. Shareholders can easily liquidate their investment. 5. Economies of scale are possible.	1. Divorce of ownership and management. 2. Diseconomies of scale, especially growth of impersonal management.

4. The Co-operative movement

This started with the Rochdale pioneers in 1844 who distributed their profits, not according to the capital invested but in proportion to members' purchases. To join a retail co-operative society a £1 share is purchased. Each member possesses one vote regardless of the number of shares held (compare with public companies). Profits are distributed to members according to their purchases by issuing dividend stamps which are redeemable for cash or added (with a bonus) to the member's share capital account. The retail societies are regionally organised. Each society elects a Committee of Management who determine policy and appoint managers to implement it. Despite their problems in the late 1950s and early 1960s the retail societies still account for 5 per cent of Britain's retail trade.

They provide the capital for the Co-operative Wholesale Society (C.W.S.) who supply them with merchandise, both food and non-food (often under their own label) and conduct national advertising campaigns. The C.W.S. own factories, farms (both at home and abroad), and is controlled by a Board of Directors elected by the retail societies. Profits are distributed to retail societies in proportion to their purchases. The whole co-operative movement is co-ordinated by the Co-operative Union to whom all the retail and wholesale societies are affiliated.

Public sector

In this sector the organisations' objectives are often social and political with less emphasis on profit maximisation. Although nationalised industries are the most well-known public organisation, many important services are provided by local authorities or directly by the State (education, defence, health, etc.).

Nationalisation

Although the British Broadcasting Corporation and the Port of London Authority were State creations, true nationalisation involves the State taking over organisations previously in private hands. The main impetus to nationalisation occurred with the advent of the Labour government in 1945 who nationalised the coal industry (1946), part of air transport (1949), railways (1947), electricity (1947), gas (1948) and iron and steel (1949). Nationalisation stems from individual Acts of Parliament which permit the Government to compulsorily purchase the existing shares for stocks in the nationalised industry. Nationalised industries are owned by the nation and financed by the Government, to whom all profits (trading surpluses) are paid and who bear any losses. Each industry is controlled by a board appointed by the relevant minister although his freedom of choice is normally circumscribed by the nationalising Act. The board is responsible for the day-to-day running, although the minister advises on general policy. Recently, however, government interference has grown, British Airways being instructed to purchase British aircraft instead of American ones. Parliament questions the minister on broad policy issues and debates nationalised industries' annual reports, thereby ensuring some public accountability. To improve accountability Consumer Councils were established in various areas (railways, gas, electricity) consisting of 20–30 unpaid members chosen by the minister. Although useful in theory their practical value is doubtful.

Arguments for nationalisation

1. Some politicians believe all forms of production should be state owned and consider this justifies nationalisation.

2. Where an industry possesses numerous firms this can result in duplication of services and harmful competition. Nationalisation enables rationalisation and economies of scale are obtained.

3. It is necessary to ensure essential services are available to all. Whilst supplying electricity to large towns is profitable, supplying isolated farmhouses is not. Private enterprise would probably only supply the former. Electricity will only be available to all at a reasonable price if provided by the State. Similar arguments apply to transport services to isolated rural communities.

4. The high capital investment required in certain industries encourages monopoly. Nationalisation is justified to protect consumers from exploitation.

5. The 'commanding heights' theory states that certain key industries (iron and steel, coal, transport, etc.) are essential to the economy and so should be state controlled.

6. Industries crucial to a nation's long-term security such as atomic energy and aerospace need nationalising because their continued existence should be independent of the profit motive.
7. Where the capital required to finance long-term capital investment is not provided by the individual investor the Government may require nationalisation before providing finance. A similar argument exists for high-risk investment areas which are essential for public security.
8. By controlling certain industries the Government can regulate economic activity. In a depression private industry may not invest, whereas a Government considering the long-term implications will base their investment decisions on social as well as economic grounds.
9. Profits are available for relief of taxpayers and not limited to a small number of shareholders.

Arguments against nationalisation

1. There is a lack of accountability in nationalised industries. If the public do not like the company's product they will not purchase them, sales will therefore fall causing a decline in profits. This will then force a review of the products which are being manufactured. Nationalised industries are less accountable to consumer demand. Even their limited parliamentary accountability may restrict managerial initiative, the consequences of a wrong decision acting as a disincentive to positive decision-making.
2. Profitability reflects a private firm's efficiency, but the dual objectives of many nationalised industries make the criterion of efficiency unacceptable. Poor management is less easily detectable and dis-economies of scale (especially growth of red-tape) can develop. The profit motive also encourages efficiency; this is lacking in nationalised industries where losses are borne by the Government.
3. Nationalisation can create a monopoly situation. One reason for nationalisation is to control monopolies but nationalisation creates monopolies and new possibilities of exploitation.
4. Nationalised industries have mixed objectives. Many nationalised industries are expected to make a profit or break-even, which clashes with their social objectives, which are often the reason for nationalisation. A railway can become profitable by axing lines to rural communities but this may be socially undesirable.
5. Government interference is another disadvantage. Governments often use nationalised industries to further their social and economic policies, jeopardising that industry's progress. They are 'forced' to accept voluntary pay and price restraint and redundancy may become impossible, because of political considerations, although overmanning loses millions of pounds daily.

Mixed enterprise

This is a public company with considerable state financial and managerial involvement, e.g. British Petroleum, British Leyland, Campbell-Laird Shipyards and Upper Clyde Shipyards. Government intervention is often necessary to revitalise ailing industries who are large exporters or are sited in areas of high unemployment.

Examination questions

1. What is the main purpose of the Annual General Meeting of a Public Limited Liability Company?

(Q. 1(a)   1977)

2. What is the maximum number of members in a partnership?

(Q. 1(f)   1976)

3. In terms of ownership, to whom are the Directors of a Joint-Stock Company responsible?

(Q. 1(h)   1976)

4. What special difficulties face the small private firm which wishes to expand?

(Q. 10   1976)

5. Briefly explain the kind of information contained in:
   (i) The Memorandum;
   (ii) The Articles of Association.

(Q. 1(d)   1975)

6. If Public Limited Companies are accountable to their shareholders, to whom are the nationalised industries accountable?

(Q. 1(i)   1975)

7. What are the main differences between Public Limited Companies and Public Corporations?

(Q. 10   1975)

8. Describe any **two** of the following forms of business enterprise:
   (i) The sole proprietor
   (ii) Partnerships
   (iii) Private companies
   (iv) Public Limited Liability companies

(Q. 12   1978)

9. Consider the strengths and weaknesses of the small business unit in today's economy.

(Q. 4   1978)

10. What are the principal ways in which business enterprises in the private sector are owned and controlled?

(Q. 5   1973)

Sample questions

1. Following the European example it may not be long before workers will be allowed to sit on the Board of Directors of a company.

(a) Since most workers will not have invested their money in the company they work for, what arguments are there for letting them have seats on the board?

(b) At the present time, to whom are the Board of Directors responsible?

2. Select a nationalised industry of your choice and examine why the service it provides, or product which it produces, needs to be supplied through public enterprise and financed from public funds.

Size of firms
Chapter 7

Growth factors

Growth may be sought to obtain the *internal economies of scale* which arise from large-scale production because by lowering the costs of production they increase profits. They can be divided into six categories:

1. Technical

Large-scale production enables the production process to be divided into specific tasks, permitting specialisation of capital and labour (division of labour). In car firms each employee performs a limited number of operations. He is more productive than his counterpart in a small workshop because by specialising in one operation he becomes more skilled at it, does not lose time switching from one task to another and requires less instruction to become a fully trained operative. Specialised equipment can be used because the volume of output enables continuous production, thereby permitting its full utilisation. Only the largest firms can purchase the sophisticated equipment operated automatically and controlled by a computer which enable man and machine to combine more effectively.

Costs of production also fall because fixed costs can be spread over more units. Research and development costs of *Concorde* were estimated at £720 million in 1972. The more *Concordes* sold the less each plane has to contribute to these costs (which are fixed and do not change with the level of production) (see Table 7.1). In publishing, the cost of setting up the type print (fixed costs) for a book is high. This must be recouped out of the selling price, hence the more a book sells the lower its price (see Table 7.2).

Tooling-up a production line is a fixed cost and the more items produced the cheaper the final price. Domestic car producers demand

Table 7.1

Planes sold	Research and Development costs (estimated) (as an element in the final price)
16	£45 million per plane
30	£24 million per plane
100	£7.2 million per plane
200	£3.6 million per plane

Table 7.2

Cost of print setting (£)	Books sold	Cost of printing/book (£)
2,500	2,000	1.25
2,500	4,000	0.62½p
2,500	6,000	0.41p
2,500	10,000	0.25p

a large and expanding home market because high sales reduce the fixed cost/item, making prices more competitive abroad.

Resources are also saved as size increases. Doubling the size of an oil tanker does not require doubling the steel, the crew or the fuel, and yet it carries double the oil. The increasing size of furnaces and chemical plant reflect the same principle.

2. Marketing

Large companies purchase raw materials in bulk, thereby obtaining favourable discounts, and high sales enable marketing costs, such as advertising, to be spread over more items. Because heavy advertising is possible the product becomes more saleable, making sales representatives more productive. The average size of each order increases whilst the time involved in obtaining the order remains relatively constant.

3. Financial

Large firms with good reputations are considered financially more secure than smaller firms and can therefore borrow money from banks and through the new-issues market, often at favourable rates of interest. Small firms who are unknown and have little collateral find fund-raising difficult, hence the creation of the National Enterprise Board. Large firms are also less prone to liquidity (cash-flow) problems. These arise because suppliers demand payment whilst debtors are slow to pay. If there is insufficient 'cash' to pay creditors they can force the company into liquidation. The large firm can 'apply' pressure on debtors to pay whilst its financial standing usually means creditors will wait. Small firms are less effective in either situation.

4. Managerial

Division of labour occurs in management as well as at operative level. The sole trader performs all the management tasks: she is a production controller, personnel officer, cost accountant, etc. whereas larger firms can fully utilise experts. By employing them it allows other managers to plan ahead, being less involved with daily problems which helps to avoid unplanned growth. Large organisations such as I.C.I. specialise even further by having management teams responsible for each division of production.

5. Risk bearing

Businesses are vulnerable if their products lose their selling appeal. Larger firms can eliminate this problem by employing business economists to forecast trends and by diversifying their products to minimise the effects of falling sales in one area. In a small firm a minor commercial set-back might result in a disaster.

6. Research

Maintaining a research and development programme involves employing highly-paid scientists and using costly equipment. Even where the 'idea' comes from a small firm the 'development' time (i.e. turning the idea into a saleable product) means heavy financial commitment in development which cannot be recouped for a considerable period. Probably only the large firm can cope with this financial burden. The larger firms are therefore more likely to discover new products, improve existing ones or discover new methods of production which lower costs.

Growth can arise by a firm expanding (internal growth) or by amalgamation with a similar business. Such an amalgamation, whether agreed or through a takeover, is called **horizontal** integration. Two builders may merge to achieve advantages of bulk buying and better utilisation of resources. British Leyland was an amalgamation of car companies such as Morris, Austin, Standard, Triumph, Rover and Jaguar. The merger may increase profits through rationalisation. The amalgamation of aerospace firms meant one research and development programme.

Firms who integrate horizontally may become more profitable by lowering their costs but the merger may also produce higher profits by creating a monopoly situation. The integrating firms can devote more resources to expansion rather than fighting off competitors and their dominance gives them greater bargaining power with suppliers and customers. A monopoly position may also be desired because it reduces the stresses caused by competition, the organisation knowing that consumers have no alternative but to purchase their products.

Growth may be sought, not to increase profitability, but to ensure survival. Competition between two large firms might be mutually harmful and so agreements could be reached on markets, pricing and common buying policies. Such arrangements are called **cartels**. Where a firm's success depends on one product it may wish to safeguard its source of supply (especially if demand is increasing) or guarantee its retail outlets (especially during economic recessions). This can be achieved by backward or forward **vertical** integration. The former involves integration with prior stages in the production process (the takeover by a tyre company of rubber plantations), whilst the latter involves integration with firms in later stages of production or distribution, such as petrol companies taking over garages.

A firm whose prosperity depends on one product is susceptible to market changes and **lateral** integration (merging of firms producing non-related products) can reduce this dependence. Tobacco firms diversified into soft drinks and other areas to compensate for possible reductions in cigarette smoking due to the severe health risks. Another motive for the formation of 'conglomerates' (the result of lateral integration) is to embrace products with wider profit margins.

Survival of the small firm

Although large firms obtain internal economies of scale, they are numerically outnumbered by small firms. These survive and prosper because:

1. Dis-economies of scale hinder large firms
(a) Larger firms dealings with their customers may become impersonal and where this is important, as with specialist retailers, the small firm can effectively compete although unable to obtain the economies of scale.
(b) Specialisation requires more co-ordination, possible increases in clerical and administrative staff with managers spending more time operating clerical procedures and less in managing.
(c) Working for large organisations may be impersonal whereas a small entrepreneur can know her staff personally. In large businesses the depersonalisation of employees and the repetitive nature of the work means delays, frustrations and industrial problems.
(d) Specialisation results in interdependence. Twelve door-hangers at The Ford Motor Company went on strike in 1977 and closed the

whole plant because all the other production operations depended on them.

(e) Large-scale production means mistakes can be more costly. The misunderstanding of market trends which resulted in the failure of tobacco-substitute cigarettes was an expensive financial disaster.

(f) Specialisation usually entails expensive production lines which require a lengthy production run to recoup the fixed costs. The inability to respond to swiftly changing demand renders it unsuitable for areas where this is flexible such as fashion manufacturing.

2. Economies of scale are unavailable

A limited market limits the possibility of specialisation. Small firms make luxury hand-made products and small builders flourish because their market is local. In other areas, such as hairdressers, doctors and solicitors where the main cost is labour, financial or technical economies cannot be achieved. The most common firm is therefore the small one.

Examination questions

1. Give an example of a process you are familiar with which illustrates 'division of labour' and explain some of the advantages and disadvantages of such a process.
   (Q. 3 1976)

2. What benefits can companies gain by forming a merger?
   (Q. 12 1976)

3. Why may large organisations be able to produce more cheaply than small ones?
   (Q. 12 1975)

4. What economic arguments can be made to justify the merging of firms?
   (Q. 8 1974)

The organisation of a firm

Chapter 8

The object of any business is to make the most efficient use of its resources. Although all businesses share this common objective, the organisation required to achieve it varies with the size and nature of the business (wholesaling, retailing, manufacturing, etc.). It is therefore misleading to talk about a common organisation structure. The following therefore relates to the structure of a typical manufacturing concern. Such a business is concerned with purchasing materials, manufacturing products and selling them. The organisation is specifically created to perform these functions.

The management activities of the firm (management functions) may be performed by one person but in large companies there are specialised departmental heads and often section heads within the departments. In large public companies, control is exercised by the Board of Directors whose functions include:

1. The protection of the shareholders' interests.
2. The determination of company policy.
3. Deciding on the proportion of profits to be distributed to shareholders.
4. The selection of the top executives.
5. Ensuring the requirements of legislation are complied with.
6. Authorisation of major capital expenditure.

The Managing Director, who sits on the board, is a full-time employee (unlike some directors who may be part-time) and translates board policy into specific objectives for his management team. His is the most senior appointment in the company and he controls senior functional managers.

The main management functions are: 1. Technical; 2. Marketing; 3. Administrative; 4. Personnel.

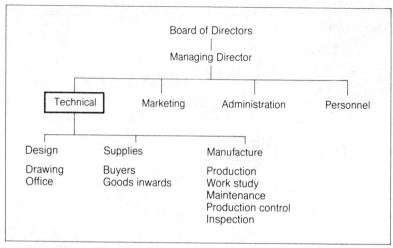

Fig. 8.1 The technical function

Technical (Fig. 8.1)

The design department supplies the manufacturing department with detailed drawings, specifications and parts list when they are satisfied with the quality of the final product. To perform this function efficiently requires liaison with marketing (the product must be saleable) and finance to ensure the design is cost-effective with the selling price producing a reasonable return on capital. The *supplies* division purchases raw materials and component parts required by the *manufacturing* division who produce the product in the most efficient manner.

The function of the manufacturing division involves employing specialists. **Industrial engineers** (work-study engineers) examine manufacturing methods and factory layout to ascertain the most efficient manufacturing methods and factory layout. Another specialist, the **production controller**, ensures the production process runs smoothly, eliminating delays and bottlenecks that arise because of shortages of materials or equipment by maintaining an adequate supply of material, machines and skilled labour. If shortages do occur she must allocate priorities, as bottlenecks cause delivery delays with an ultimate loss of orders and a decrease in productivity. The production controller liaises with the **plant engineer** who maintains the plant, regularly servicing it, and provides a skilled team to repair machines that break down on the production line. The machine operators in a section are responsible to a foreman who co-ordinates their efforts to achieve maximum productivity. She is usually responsible to a superintendent. The final stage in the manufacturing function is product inspection (quality control) which attempts to see that no defective products reach the consumer, thereby damaging the firm's image.

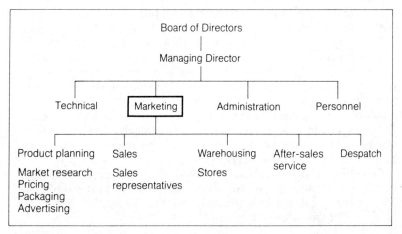

Fig. 8.2 The marketing (or commercial) function

Marketing (Fig. 8.2)

The marketing (or commercial) function attempts to discover consumer needs, find a suitable product, persuade the consumers to purchase it and then ensure it is available for sale. Most of the functions are illustrated in the marketing of a new product from its inception to final sale. A broad specification is made for a new product and a sample survey of potential customers is conducted to assess sales potential. If the initial soundings are satisfactory a design sample is produced, detailed estimates made on cost, sales potential, etc. and the packaging is designed. To test the product's impact it will be marketed in a 'sample' area. If the pilot sales figures are encouraging preparations will commence for a national launch.

The national launching is usually preceded by extensive advertising aimed at 'selling' the product. This has become so important that even large firms may employ outside advertising agencies to plan their campaigns. Advertising can be through the local press, national television, free gifts, sports sponsorship, etc. with the choice depending on the company's size and the nature of the market. I.C.I. would advertise a new fertiliser in a farmer's magazine whilst a record company would advertise new 'singles' in a teenagers' magazine. Allied to the advertising campaign is the packaging of the product. Where it is for display in retail outlets this must possess sales appeal but the packaging must be sufficiently strong to withstand the buffeting it may receive during the distribution chain. A crushed packet of biscuits will remain unsold no matter how attractive the packaging. It must also comply with legal requirements such as those prescribed by the Trade Descriptions Act (1968) or by foreign legislation if the product is for export.

Having designed a product which the public wants, the marketing function must ensure it is available in retail outlets. A shopkeeper cannot sell goods she does not have in stock. Warehouses are required to hold stocks and an efficient distribution network is required to deliver them to the retailers. The long-term success of a company, however, depends on producing 'satisfied' customers who remain loyal to the company products. To retain customer goodwill an efficient after-sales service must exist (with spares available for older models). This is especially true when the products are mechanical. Many firms also provide a guarantee to supplement the protection provided by the Sale of Goods Act (as amended).

Once the product has been launched, the sales representatives obtain orders and arrange deliveries to customers within their regions. They make regular sales returns and by monitoring these and comparing them with competitors' sales the market research department can assess the viability of existing products, pinpointing weaknesses and strengths which help other specialists formulate the correct 'sales policy'.

Fig. 8.3 The administrative function

Administrative (Fig. 8.3)

The *clerical and secretarial* services in a small firm are usually provided centrally. In larger firms many are decentralised, each department possessing its own secretarial and office staff responsible for the day-to-day running of the department, typing of letters, keeping of records, etc. Even though decentralisation occurs, some services such as reprographic and the post room may continue to be operated on a centralised basis.

The *financial* services fall into three main categories. Management (or financial accounting) is usually the responsibility of a **financial accountant** and involves monitoring performance and the return on capital. She provides her management colleagues with information on costs, profits, cash flow and other financial data. Without an early-warning system cash-flow problems could arise, causing a financial crisis or even bankruptcy (as occurred with Rolls Royce). A firm can possess a healthy order book, a reasonable cost structure but because of cash-flow problems insufficient cash to pay its suppliers and workforce. Budgetary control is the responsibility of a **cost accountant**. Before each financial year, functional heads estimate their expenditure for that year. A budget is constructed based on these and the cost accountant monitors expenditure and advises functional heads who appear to be in danger of overspending. Anyone overspending is answerable to the cost accountant, who may be allowed to authorise overspending in exceptional circumstances. Although wages may be paid direct into employees' bank accounts the wages office, under the control of the **cashier**, calculates gross and net wages (i.e. calculates stoppages such as tax and national insurance). In addition she is responsible for paying for the purchase of small items out of petty cash.

The final administrative function is the *legal*, usually under the **company secretary**. The legal section is responsible for ensuring the law is complied with, it may undertake legal work such as the drawing up of contracts and it advises functional heads on the practical implementation of legislation such as the Employment Protection Act and the Health and Safety at Work Act. The growing complexity of modern legislation has resulted in an increased use of outside specialists to advise on legal matters.

Personnel (Fig. 8.4)

The powers of personnel departments depend on the organisation. In some, the senior personnel officer possesses only an advisory role whilst in others she possesses a seat on the board and full executive powers. Figure 8.4 illustrates the functions of a typical personnel department.

Being responsible for staff *recruitment*, the personnel department must assess the future needs of the organisation. Manpower planning involves estimating the staff required at a future date and then, by deducting employees leaving the firm through natural wastage (retirement) and other causes (dismissal, promotion), ascertaining the numbers that need to be recruited. Having estimated future manpower requirements, recruitment and training can be planned so that the firm possesses sufficient skilled labour. In addition to recruiting and

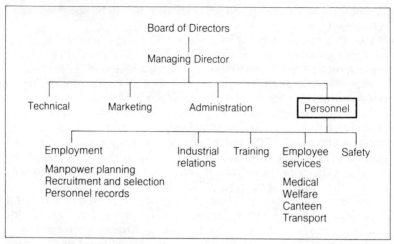

Fig. 8.4 The personnel function

selecting staff, they complete the necessary paperwork and deal with promotions and transfers. Where employees prove unsatisfactory the personnel department might dismiss them or advise the department concerned.

The *industrial relations* section negotiates with unions over conditions of service, disputes, stoppages, redundancies, etc. and its importance has led many firms to employ an industrial relations expert. Because of the importance of legislation, those involved require a working knowledge of relevant Acts including the Employment Protection Act and Contracts of Employment Act. The

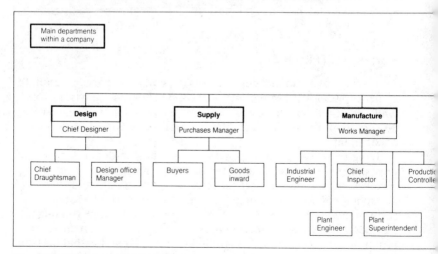

Fig. 8.5 Main departments within a company

next broad area of responsibility is *education and training* (see Chapter 4).

Employee services include providing medical services, recreational and canteen facilities and, if the firm is ill-served by public transport, perhaps coaches for the workforce. The final function of employee services is *safety* although since the Health and Safety at Work Act has imposed criminal liability on employers many firms have transferred this to a separate department. The responsibility for safety means maintaining a safe system of work and extends to heating, lighting, ventilation and accident prevention.

Although the above gives an outline of the main functions within a business organisation many variations are found. There may be a separate computer department providing administrative and technical services to the other departments and it requires emphasising that organisations are designed to fulfil objectives, and as these vary between firms so will their organisations. The main departments and department heads within a company are shown in Fig. 8.5.

Examination questions

1. A company about to market a new product had a management meeting to develop a check list of all the factors to be considered before finally putting the product on the market. The first two items on the check list were:
   (*a*) Quality
   (*b*) Cost
       Discuss the importance of these two factors and consider **three** other factors of importance in the successful marketing of a new product.
                                                  (Q. 3   1977)

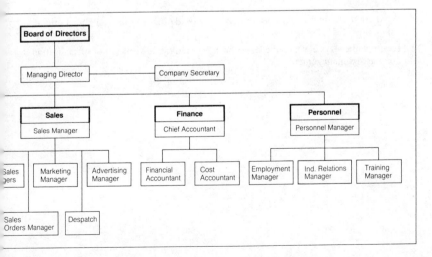

2. The A.B. Company Ltd. has just marketed a new product with disappointing results. Give **four** possible reasons for the poor sales figures.

(Q. 5 1975)

3. Discuss **four** ways in which the marketing function can contribute to the success of a business.

(Q. 9 1978)

4. A large organisation is able to make full use of division of labour amongst managers.

Board of Directors

|

Managing Director

Chief Accountant   Personnel Manager   Etc.

(*a*) Draw an organisation chart similar to that above, simply illustrating the main functions of any large organisation.

(*b*) Write briefly on each of the main functions and their importance to the organisation.

(*c*) Briefly highlight **one** main disadvantage which may result from such managerial specialisation.

(Q. 11 1977)

Sample questions

1. The main management functions of a business are **technical**, **commercial** or **marketing**, **administrative** and **personnel**.

Select any **two** functions and examine the contribution which they make to the success of a business.

2. In recent years many of the functions performed by **line** management have been given to specialist functions such as **personnel**. Examine the role of the **personnel** department, identifying their main areas of work.

3. 'In the large public company there is a divorce of ownership from control.' Explain this statement.

4. What are the main functions performed by a Board of Directors in a Public Limited Company?

5. Examine the ways in which the larger business employs the concept of specialisation amongst its management.

Sources of finance
Chapter 9

To the individual

An individual requiring finance for the purchase of consumer items possesses numerous sources. Finance is available through budget accounts operated by many leading retailers. The customer pays a fixed monthly sum, for example £10, regardless of purchases. In return she is immediately entitled to credit facilities up to 6, 12 or 24 times her monthly payment. If it were 24, her credit would commence at £240 and she could purchase goods until her outstanding debt reaches £240. The system is one of revolving credit, and each month her credit would rise by £10 providing no purchases are made (see Table 9.1).

Table 9.1 Revolving credit

Month	Payment in	Purchases	Outstanding credit
1	10	—	240
2	10	—	250 (240+10)
3	10	90	170 (250+10−90)
4	10		180 (170+10)
5	10	190	(180+10−190)

Individuals requiring finance for lengthier periods might choose hire-purchase. The buyer obtains the goods on payment of a deposit, agreeing to pay the balance (plus interest) by weekly or monthly instalments over a fixed period, obtaining ownership on payment of the *last* instalment. Until then the goods remain the property of the vendor and can be repossessed after certain legal formalities have been complied with. Sales of television sets, deep freezers, washing machines and other consumer durables are often financed this way. The rate of interest charged depends on the general level of interest rates but certain safeguards have been introduced by the Consumer Credit Act (1977). A modified version of hire-purchase is the credit sale agreement where the purchaser obtains ownership on payment of the first instalment. If the customer defaults before paying the final instalment the vendor cannot repossess the goods, only sue for the sum outstanding. The credit sale agreement is mainly used for items of little resale value. For both parties to a hire-purchase transaction there are advantages and disadvantages, some of which are detailed in Table 9.2.

Table 9.2   Advantages and disadvantages of hire-purchase

Advantages	Disadvantages
(a) Consumer	
1. Makes the purchase of expensive consumer durables possible.	1. More expensive than a cash purchase because of the interest.
2. Overcomes the possibility of inflation increasing the item's price.	2. No legal ownership until payment of final instalment. The purchaser cannot resell items.
3. The purchaser obtains immediate use of the items purchased.	3. Danger of the purchaser over-committing herself.
4. During the period of payment the retailer is responsible for defects.	4. Illness or unemployment could result in instalments not being paid and forfeiture of goods.
(b) Retailer	
1. Retains contact with customer, hence possibility of further sales.	1. Greater possibility of bad debts.
2. Increases sales of expensive items.	2. Goods repossessed may be unfit for re-sale.
3. If she acts as an intermediary between the finance company and consumer she receives a commission.	3. Increased paperwork.
	4. The legal formalities to be complied with before repossession is possible.

Where the retailer cannot finance the credit a third party (the finance company) is involved. The retailer legally sells the goods to the finance company who resell them to the customer. This is, however, a paper transaction and the retailer sells to the customer in the normal way.

Somebody requiring funds for a continental holiday would find the above sources unsuitable. She requires cash, repayable over a period of time. This may be obtainable from her bank or insurance company who may advance cash against an endowment policy.

House purchasers are unlikely to possess sufficient funds for a cash purchase and the size and duration of the necessary loan makes a bank loan inappropriate. The main suppliers of finance are building societies, who are bodies registered under the friendly societies legislation. They provide loans, giving priority to their own investors, for up to 30 years to cover 70–90 per cent of their valuation of the property. The percentage depends on the property's age, its construction and marketability. Its value is assessed by the building society's surveyor (the mortgagee paying the cost) and is usually below the purchase price. Hence the prospective mortgagee will require several thousand pounds deposit.

When determining the amount of the loan the society consider the applicant's ability to repay it. Hence it depends on age, annual salary (which may sometimes include overtime and commission) of the applicant and possibly their spouse. The maximum loan is usually $2\frac{1}{2}$ times income. Interest paid attracts tax relief; therefore part of the mortgage's cost is paid by the Inland Revenue! If the mortgage rate is 9 per cent the borrower effectively pays nearer 6 per cent. On receiving the mortgage, the mortgagee deposits the property's title deeds with the building society as security and insures the property. If she defaults (fails to pay) the society can foreclose, i.e. sell the house and deduct the amount due, handing over any surplus to the borrower. Normally, however, societies attempt to help borrowers in difficulty.

The societies' lending is determined by deposits and to encourage investors they offer three main types of account.

1. Paid-up share account. Each £1 investment purchases a fully paid-up share on which interest is earned. Withdrawals are normally paid on demand except for substantial sums when a short period of notice may be required. This is the most common method of investing.
2. Monthly saving plan ('Build-up shares', etc.) For investors prepared to save regularly, a higher rate of interest is paid. The investor agrees to save a fixed sum each month (£1–£50) and then makes regular deposits. Part withdrawals are forbidden but the account may be closed without penalty and interest is payable until the date of withdrawal.
3. An investor prepared to leave her savings untouched for two (or three) years obtains a higher rate of interest than for a paid-up share account. The minimum investment is £500. After two (or three) years the savings, with interest, are automatically repaid.

   The societies also operate save-as-you-earn schemes. All their interest rates are free of income tax and interest is calculated on a daily basis, accruing to the original investment every half year. The total investment in a building society is limited and, unlike the commercial banks, the building societies open on Saturdays.

The rate charged to mortgagees (which may fluctuate during the course of the mortgage) is approximately 2 per cent above that offered to investors. The latter is determined by other interest rates (especially the **Minimum Lending Rate**), the building society rates competing with those offered by banks, etc.

To businesses

The small-businesswoman usually obtains the finance to start trading from her savings or, if she belongs to a partnership or small company, the savings of her partners. Additional temporary finance may be obtained by:

(*a*)   a loan from the local bank;

(*b*)   a loan from a finance company. This is usually more expensive than a bank loan because a higher rate of interest is charged;

(*c*)   arranging, or extending, credit with her suppliers.

Where additional capital is required and retained profits are insufficient, the capital may be obtained from a bank or finance house, or by changing the type of business organisation. If the capital involved is considerable it might be necessary to go 'public'. The costs of going public may be prohibitive for a medium-size company (a public issue of shares is expensive and it is uneconomic to raise less than £500,000) and it may therefore be forced to request finance from the N.E.B. (see p. 60, Finance corporations).

The larger company can go public and raise long-term capital by issuing shares to the general public who then become part-owners of the business and receive a share of the profits. Their liability is limited to the amount they have subscribed, or agreed to subscribe, on the shares. They possess limited liability and if the company goes bankrupt the creditors cannot seize their personal property.

A large company can obtain additional temporary finance (i.e. for less than twelve months) through:

(*a*)   a bank overdraft, large companies often negotiating preferential rates of interest;

(*b*)   obtaining a longer period of credit from their suppliers.

A permanent increase in capital can come from:

(*i*)   *Retained profits.*   These have traditionally been a major source of capital; between 1950–72 they accounted for 40 per cent of 'new capital', but their importance has declined due to falling profit levels. The pre-tax rate of return on capital employed in UK manufacturing industries has fallen from 11.4 per cent in 1964 to less than 4 per cent.

(*ii*)   Calling up any uncalled capital still outstanding.

(*iii*)   *Issuing new shares.*   If this necessitates an increase in the amount of the authorised capital the permission of the Registrar of Companies is required. The New Issues market exists for securities being sold for the first time. It is controlled by the merchant banks, of whom approximately 50 are members of the Issuing Houses Association, who link investors with surplus cash and companies requiring additional capital. The merchant banks advise companies when to float the issue and at which price. A new issue can be made in four ways. An **offer for sale** entails the issuing house, probably a merchant bank, offering shares to the public at a fixed price. The offer is advertised in the 'serious' press and a prospectus is published with an application form. The prospectus, a requirement of the Companies Act (1948), must include information on the company's history, details of directors, details of the issue, profit statements for the last ten years and details of dividends paid. Although of little use to the individual investor, it enables the financial press to assess realistically the share price. On the closing date shares are allocated to successful applicants; if it is oversubscribed applications are scaled down and/or a ballot is held to determine successful applicants. Where it is undersubscribed the unallotted shares are taken up by the underwriters who will place them in the future. The minimum value of shares offered must normally exceed £500,000 with not more than 10 per cent being reserved for preferential applicants.

Placings involve a City institution, such as a merchant bank, buying the shares and placing them with certain large institutional investors or companies. Placings are primarily used for small issues. **Prospectus issue** is rare and involves the company selling shares direct to the public without the assistance of an issuing house. This method is mainly limited to the issue of government stocks. The final method is the **rights issue** which means issuing new shares to existing shareholders for cash, each shareholder being offered one share for each share, or number of shares, she holds at a favourable price.

(iv) Issuing debentures or unsecured loan stock.   These pay a fixed rate of interest and the former is secured against the firm's assets. A failure to pay the interest could result in the firm's bankruptcy. The type of stock issued (equity, debenture, etc.) depends on the level of interest rates and the state of the stock market. Where share prices are high (bull market) an issue of ordinary shares may be favourable. Because investors are anxious to buy shares they accept lower yields and higher P/E ratios (multiple of last published earnings per share represented by current price), thus enabling the issue price to be higher. When the market is depressed (bear market) it may be advantageous to issue loan stock, especially if interest rates are low.

(v) Bank loans.   In 1977 banks' total lending to the manufacturing sector of industry was £8,549 million. Where a small business with little collateral requires a large capital sum for expansion (venture capital) it may obtain this from a merchant bank in return for a block of its shares. Although this is a high-risk investment, one success will offset numerous failures.

(vi) Mortgaging company property to a finance corporation or bank.   The loan is repaid, with interest, over a period of years.

(vii) Finance corporations.   The most important are jointly owned by the leading City institutions and have Government backing. Examples are Finance for Industry Ltd. and The Agricultural Mortgage Corporation Ltd. (specialising in loans to farmers). The newest body created to help finance industry is the National Enterprise Board.

The N.E.B. was formed in November 1975 to supplement the existing sources of finance to industry and in particular to two sectors. The first was the public company unable to float a new issue because of a poor past record and the private company unable to afford the costs of going 'public'. The second was the small company (employing less than 200 staff) requiring risk capital. In the manufacturing sector this latter group number 70,000 and they are 'a source of innovation in products, techniques and services . . . the traditional breeding ground for new industries and the seed-bed from which new large companies will grow to challenge and stimulate the established leaders of industry.' (Bolton Committee). Although some institutions specifically cater for small firms (The Industrial and Commercial Finance Corporation) the majority of small companies are unable to obtain finance.

The N.E.B. comprises a full-time chairman, deputy chairman and 9 part-time members who are assisted by over 70 staff (divided between London and the regions). In addition, part-time regional boards have been created. Board members are appointed by the Secretary of State for Industry who is also empowered to determine the financial duties of the N.E.B. and issue general or specific directives (subject to the provisions of the Industry Act, 1975). In practice, Government supervision is general, allowing the N.E.B. considerable freedom in its day-to-day operations. Its funds come from the National Loans Fund, on which interest is paid, and in the form of dividend capital, voted by Parliament, on which a dividend may be payable.

In general objectives are to:

(a) develop and assist the UK economy;
(b) promote industrial efficiency and international competitiveness;
(c) provide, maintain or safeguard productive employment.

In practice this means:

(i) promoting companies who export or manufacture import-substitutes;
(ii) improving employment in areas of high unemployment;
(iii) encouraging developments in advanced technology.

The N.E.B. operates by providing advisory services, loans (at commercial rates) or by purchasing the company's equity, the latter being the main method of supplying long-term finance (especially risk capital) for manufacturing firms. Although requiring an adequate return on investments – it cannot provide cheap loans and its actions must be commercially sound – it takes a wider view of national benefits and opportunities, paying especial attention to export implications and the need to promote Government industrial policy. Some of the main financial activities of the N.E.B. are listed in Table 9.3.

Table 9.3 N.E.B. shareholdings and loans

Company	% of shares held by N.E.B.	Cost (£)
British Leyland	98.9	515,910,000
Bull Motors Ltd.	100	500,000
Data Recording Instrument Co. Ltd.	63.1	3,977,000
Ferranti	50.0	6,000,000
Rolls-Royce Ltd.	100	196,000,000
United Medical Enterprises	70.0	5,774,000
Barrow Hepburn Group Ltd.	4.1	450,000
Loans 31 May 1978 (selected)	**(£)**	
British Leyland	165,581,000	
Cambridge Instrument Co. Ltd.	2,000,000	
Herbert Ltd.	5,705,000	
Rolls-Royce Ltd.	84,264,000	
Total loans to all companies = 264,449,000		

The Board is not involved in the day-to-day management of companies but requires progress reports to ensure profitability levels are acceptable. It ensures the management teams are effective and overhauls management systems where necessary. It does insist on discussing future plans and where it possesses a majority holding it must approve them. There may also be provision for an N.E.B. director or directors.

To local government

Capital necessary to run municipal enterprises is usually provided by borrowing. If the central Government approves the loan the authority can borrow the money from the Government or the public. Whichever source is used the loan must be repaid out of the enterprise's profits or through the rates.

To State enterprises

These include British Rail, British Airways and the National Coal Board. Where retained profits are insufficient for capital development the enterprise must request a loan from the Government who will obtain the necessary finance from the taxpayer or by issuing gilt-edge securities.

Examination questions

1. Other than through issuing shares, what are the main ways a large public limited company can raise finance?

   (Q. 7   1977)

2. Imagine you are about to purchase your first house. You pay a visit to a building society or a bank to discuss the possibility of obtaining a mortgage. What are the likely questions the manager will want answered before granting your request?

   (Q. 2   1976)

3. How does a building society function? Why does a change in commercial bank interest rates affect a building society's deposit rate, and the interest rate charged on mortgages?

   (Q. 7   1974)

4. (*a*) What is the essential difference between buying goods on hire-purchase and for cash?

   (*b*) List **four** main advantages and **four** main disadvantages of buying goods through hire-purchase.

   (Q. 7 · 1978)

5. A business that needs extra capital may obtain it from a number of different sources. Describe **three** possible sources discussing the merits and drawbacks of each method.

   (Q. 6   1974)

Banking services

Chapter 10

Available to individuals

1. Savers

Anybody with surplus funds can earn interest by opening a **deposit** account. Seven days' notice is required before money can be withdrawn (and cheques cannot be drawn on such accounts) but it is normal practice for banks to waive this period of notice. Although interest is paid the capital sum invested remains unchanged. A **savings** account, specially introduced for the young saver, is a method of accumulating small amounts.

To increase her savings, securities (stocks and shares) may be purchased. Banks will advise on share portfolios and buy and sell securities on their customers' behalf. Banks also run their own unit trusts. Shares can depreciate in value and valuables might be bought as a hedge against inflation. The bank will undertake their safe deposit, although insurance is the depositor's responsibility.

2. Payers

With **current** accounts cash is repayable on demand but no interest is paid. The issue of a cheque book removes the need to carry large sums of cash but a fee is charged for each current account transaction unless the customer retains a certain balance in her account. At regular intervals a 'bank statement' is sent with details of all deposits and withdrawals. Cheques, not being legal tender, can be refused and to ensure their acceptability banks provide **cheque cards** to their customers. Providing the customer's signature matches that on the cheque card it guarantees payment of cheques up to £50. The card also allows the holder to cash cheques in Europe as well as in other branches. Where a cheque is unacceptable the customer can obtain a **bank draft** (Fig. 10.1) which is a cheque drawn on the bank. It is as good as cash.

A customer can pay several bills by one cheque through a **credit transfer** (Bank Giro). One cheque is written for the total amount with instructions regarding its division; the bank then credits each creditor's account with the appropriate sum.

A **standing order** is an instruction from the customer requesting the bank periodically to make fixed payments on her behalf. It can be used to pay an annual subscription, the monthly payment of rates, an insurance premium, etc. and removes the possibility of the customer forgetting to pay. A variant on this is a **direct debit**; the customer instructs her bank to pay any bills (sometimes up to a specified amount) submitted by a named individual. A direct debit, unlike a standing order, is available even though the bill or the interval between payments varies.

Many regular household bills (gas, electricity, telephone, etc.) are difficult to calculate. To assist the customer to save enough to pay these the bank provides **budget accounts**. The yearly total of 'regular' bills is estimated and divided by twelve. Each month this sum is transferred from the customer's current to her budget account. Bills are paid by cheques drawn on the latter account, which can be overdrawn. A fee is paid for this service with an additional charge for overdrafts incurred.

The customer requiring cash outside banking hours can, if she possesses a **cash card**, use the cash-dispensing machines sited outside many banks. Banks also provide foreign currency or travellers' cheques and assist in the transference of funds overseas through mail or cable transfer or by Foreign Draft.

The growth of **credit cards** enables bank customers to purchase goods on credit. Retailers in the scheme allow them to sign for goods or services purchased. The bill is paid by the bank (less their commission) who send the customer a monthly statement of her expenditure. A minimum monthly payment is required and interest is paid on the balance outstanding. No interest is charged if bills are settled within one month. Examples of credit cards, which are issued free, are Access and Barclaycard.

Whilst some of the above are income-producing the banks' main income arises from providing loans or overdrafts.

3. Debtors

Loans entail the bank lending a fixed sum, perhaps £500, which is credited to the customer's account. There is a fixed rate of interest and a regular repayment arrangement. An **overdraft** arises when the customer is allowed to overdraw her current account by a specified amount. Funds can be withdrawn up to the agreed limit without any further reference. Interest is paid on the sum overdrawn, which must be repaid by an agreed date, and not on the overdraft facility allowed. The differences between loans and overdrafts are explained further in

Table 10.1 Differences between loans and overdrafts

Loan	Overdraft
1. Obtained for a specified period.	Unspecified.
2. Available to persons without a bank account.	Account essential.
3. Fixed repayments.	Irregular.
4. Higher interest than overdraft.	
5. Interest usually paid on amount borrowed.	Interest paid on sum outstanding.
6. Fixed amount.	Variable amount up to a maximum.
7. Lent for longer periods than overdrafts.	Usually granted for a maximum of twelve months.

Table 10.1. Where more substantial borrowing is required, perhaps in connection with house purchase, a bridging loan may be available. A breakdown of loans and advances provided by banks to different groups in the community is shown in Table 10.2.

Table 10.2 Loans + advances

	1972 (£m.)	1977 (£m.)	197 (£m.)
Manufacturing industries	4,773	8,549	
Construction industries	1,857	3,946	
Property, hire-purchase, etc.	3,393	7,119	
Distribution, service, professional	3,111	11,096	
Personal	2,641	4,245	
Overseas residents	7,879	5,790	
Total	23,654	40,745	

Before banks will lend money they must ensure it will be repaid. Although some loans are 'unsecured', the bank relying on the borrower's personal undertaking to repay, most require the borrower to provide security (collateral). This can be securities, title deeds to property or a life insurance policy (providing it possesses a surrender value); where these are unavailable the bank may accept a guarantee from another individual, or individuals, that they will pay the debt should the borrower default.

Banks also provide miscellaneous services; helping individuals complete income tax returns, advising on capital gains tax, acting as executors on a customer's death and advising on trusts and settlements. Insurance cover may be affected through banks, whose brokers will advise on the best policies, and many banks offer pension scheme facilities.

Available to business

1. Merchant banks

Although conducting some ordinary banking business, merchant banks primarily provide services for the business community including the provision of short- and medium-term finance. They help finance overseas trade through 'acceptance credit' which enables the seller or exporter to obtain cash on shipment of the goods whilst allowing the buyer or importer to pay on their receipt (or later). This is achieved through Bills of Exchange. The purchaser (X) initiates a bill promising to pay the seller £5,000 in, for example, 60 days. The seller can obtain earlier payment by selling the bill on the discount market for £4,900. The bill's purchaser holds it for 60 days before presenting it to X for payment. Her profit for discounting the bill is £100. Bills will only be discounted where final payment is certain; if the purchaser's (X's) financial standing is unknown it will require acceptance (guaranteeing) by somebody with financial standing, such as a merchant bank. By promising payment after 60 days (for which it charges a commission) the bank ensures the bill's saleability.

Where longer-term finance is required the bank will help raise funds by public offerings or private placements of new securities. After analysing their client's financial requirements they will ensure the issue is offered on the most advantageous terms to the company.

Merchant banks act as advisers and negotiators for companies involved in mergers, takeovers and acquisitions by conducting company analysis, target selection and the formal negotiations. They also advise on the most profitable areas of investment; this 'reserve asset' facility (i.e. where to invest surplus cash) is also available to central banks, especially of emergent nations, and pension funds. In addition they provide comprehensive advisory services on fund transfers and purchase of foreign securities.

2. Commercial banks

These are primarily concerned with small and medium-sized businesses and the provision of short-term working capital. Where a temporary financial problem exists, perhaps due to delays in receiving payments, they will discount bills of exchange or provide overdraft facilities. Banks will also assist businesses to collect their debts. The bank 'buys' the firm's debts and is responsible for credit control and debt collection. This service is known as '**factoring**'. Where expansion cannot be self-financed a medium- or long-term loan may be available for periods between two and five years. Customers dealing abroad can be advised on the currency situation, exchange controls and on services provided by the Export Credits Guarantee Department. Banks also provide a free business advisory service to customers. A bank executive spends a short period with the firm and advises on costing and pricing, budgeting, cash-flow forecasting, capital investment appraisal and asset management. Banks also publish numerous advisory booklets such as 'Understanding annual accounts' and 'Improving your financial control'.

Examination questions

1. In one particular month a young couple found themselves in financial difficulties due to gas, electric and telephone bills coinciding with a repair on the car, renewal of the road fund tax, annual subscription to the R.A.C. and TV licence. The bank manager, having assured himself that their joint income was sufficient to meet their outgoings, advised them of two services which the bank offered which would help them to avoid this problem in the future.
   Describe the **two** most appropriate banking services to help this couple.
   (Q. 2   1977)

2. What is the essential difference between hire-purchase and a bank loan?
   (Q. 1(g)   1976)

3. A relative who is purchasing a car cannot decide between hire-purchase, a bank loan or a bank overdraft as the means of financing this acquisition. Explain each option to him giving guidance as to the advantages and disadvantages of each method of finance.
   (Q. 7   1975)

4. Explain simply what the term 'collateral' means in banking.
   (Q. 1(i)   1978)

   Selecting **three** of the following pairs, explain their difference in meaning:
    (i) commercial banks and merchant banks;
    (ii) loans and overdrafts;
    (iii) standing orders and credit transfers;
    (iv) deposit accounts and current accounts.
   (Q. 5   1978)

5. A friend is able to save a pound or two each week from her wages and tells you that she is saving for another 18 months when she is due to get married. She has already saved £190 which she keeps at home in a drawer. Give her advice on **three** alternative ways she can save in a more productive and secure manner.
   (Q. 8   1978)

6. Outline the main services offered by the commercial banks and explain briefly features of their operation which distinguish them from other forms of commercial enterprise.
   (Q. 11   1974)

The Stock Exchange
Chapter 11

Stock exchanges are highly organised and regulated markets for the buying and selling of second-hand quoted securities. They exist all over the world, in Paris, Brussels, Amsterdam, Zurich, New York and other cities. In Britain in 1972 the London and Provincial Stock Exchanges were combined under the title 'The Stock Exchange'. The largest exchange is in London with provincial exchanges in Glasgow, Liverpool, Manchester, Birmingham, Bristol, Edinburgh, York, Belfast and Dublin.

The London Exchange

This possesses over 4,000 elected members who are over 21, have served three years with a member firm and passed a qualifying examination. The members are grouped in approximately 300 firms of whom approximately 20 are 'jobbers'. Over 9,000 securities are listed on the Stock Exchange representing the major British companies and over 400 overseas companies. In addition to equities, the Stock Exchange deals in Government securities which account for 75 per cent of their turnover.

The Exchange is used by four main groups – individuals, companies, institutions, and Government.

1. Individuals

An individual wishing to invest part of her savings may purchase stocks and shares. The Stock Exchange Council, which regulates the conduct of members, will attempt to ensure an investor is not misled or defrauded. If any member goes bankrupt they will pay her creditors from their compensation fund and where conduct of a quoted company is questionable, dealings in its shares will be suspended pending the results of investigations.

Private investors must purchase shares through a broker.

Broker
A broker (or her authorised clerk) conducts transactions on the investor's behalf with 'jobbers' sited on the Stock Exchange floor, in addition to offering investment advice, providing research material, engaging in underwriting activities and trust management. As only brokers have access to jobbers and their numbers are controlled by the Stock Exchange Council (effectively controlled by brokers) they possess oligopolistic power. In addition they determine their own commission charges. This has led to criticism and the creation of a system which eliminates brokers.

ARIEL (Automated Real Time Investments Exchange) is a computerised system enabling those wishing to buy and sell shares to communicate directly, thereby eliminating the broker. Because of minimum charges it is mainly for the large institutional investor. Whilst ARIEL has limitations computerised dealing systems exist which completely dispense with 'trading floors'.

The broker wishing to buy or sell shares contacts a jobber.

Jobber
The jobber buys and sells securities on her own account. Each jobber specialises in one market sector and will quote two prices, the lower being the price she will pay for shares and the higher that at which she will sell. The difference is the **jobber's turn**. When the broker has obtained the best terms a 'bargain' is struck for settlement on account day.

Each party to the transaction makes a note and these are checked the following day by the respective clerks. A few days later the broker's client will receive a **contract note** showing:

(a) the price;
(b) the amount of the broker's commission;
(c) the amount of the contract stamp duty;
(d) the amount of the transfer stamp.

On settlement day the client pays (or receives) the amount stated on the contract note. Final settlement is completed by the computer network called TALISMAN (Transfer Accounting, Lodgement for Investors, Stock Management for Jobbers). The seller signs a transfer deed which, with the share certificate, is sent to the company office so the Share Register can be altered. The old certificate is cancelled and a new one sent to the purchaser.

The jobber who has purchased shares will attempt to resell them within the account period (and vice versa). Until then she is 'at risk' (i.e. she might have to hold the shares which may then fall below the purchase price), and she will therefore wish to 'close her position by a bargain the other way'. The risk is, however, minimised by the account system whereby two weeks' dealings are combined for a single settlement falling on the eleventh day (Tuesday) after the dealing period closes. This gives the jobber a better chance of balancing her books than if settlement were on a daily basis.

Account 1. opens Monday 1 Oct.
            closes Friday 12 Oct.
                        Settlement day 23 Oct.

Account 2. opens Monday 15 Oct.
            closes Friday 26 Oct.
                        Settlement day 6 Nov.

If the jobber purchases 600 units of share XYZ on 2 October and sells 200 on 8 October and 400 on 11 October, all the transactions are settled on 23 October. The proceeds of the two sales will pay for the purchase. The remainder is the jobber's profit.

The type of security purchased depends on the return sought. Where regular interest with little risk is required the investor will probably purchase: 1. Gilt-edge securities; 2. Debenture/Loan stock; 3. Preference shares.

(i) Gilt-edge securities. These are issued by the Government for a fixed period of time and carry a fixed rate of interest. They are a secure investment but will not keep pace with inflation, although when interest rates fall they can increase in value.

Example:
Four per cent consolidated stock. Par value £100.
Therefore each holder of £100 (nominal/par value) receives £4 (4%) interest annually. If interest rates rise to 8 per cent then £100 of stock sells at £50 because the £4 interest would give an 8 per cent yield.
If interest rates fall to 2 per cent the stock would have to sell at £200 to produce a 2 per cent return.

(ii) Debentures/loan stock. Loan capital and debenture stocks are issued by companies in multiples of £1, £5 or £100 and are transferable on the Stock Exchange. They are repayable on a certain date and provide a fixed rate of interest based on their par value. Debentures are secured on the company's assets and a trustee is appointed. If a proposal is considered prejudicial to debenture holders the trustee may require them to be consulted. If the company defaults on interest payments the trustee can sell the charged property and recoup the debt, handing over the balance to the company. Debentures may be secured against particular assets or there may be a floating charge over all the assets. They are one of the safest forms of investment.

Unsecured loan stock is a loan not secured against assets. Although their repayment takes priority over ordinary and preference shares (see below) they rank after secured loans. Trustees are appointed to perform the functions explained above.

A modified form of loan stock is the convertible unsecured loan which permits the investor to convert his holding from loan capital into equities on prearranged terms within a set period.

(iii) Preference shares. These are usually issued in units of £1 and are quoted on the Stock Exchange. They receive a fixed dividend expressed as a percentage of the par value.

Example:
Seven per cent preference share of £1 means 7p interest is payable on every share. If the rate of interest rises to 14 per cent the share with par value of £1 would sell at 50p. If it falls to 3.5 per cent the share would sell at £2.

Preference shares have first claim on company profits available for distribution. If a company goes into liquidation their repayment takes priority over ordinary shares (see below) but preference shareholders usually lack voting rights. A **cumulative preference share** has prior claim on the profits for current dividend and also for any arrears of dividend not paid in previous years. In limited circumstances their shareholders may obtain voting rights. Other preference shares are **participating preference shares** which entitle the shareholder to a proportion of the profits, and **redeemable preference shares** which are the only shares a company can repurchase. Whilst preference shares are usually a safe investment the interest payable may be low and they lose their real value.

Example:
Cost of preference share £100, dividend £7, inflation 10 per cent. Value of share remains constant providing interest rates remain unchanged. Loss in real value of 10 per cent.

The individual prepared to take a calculated risk may find an investment more capable of retaining, or possibly increasing, its real value.

Ordinary shares (equities). The ordinary shareholder owns the company, each share entitling the holder to an equal share of the profits (hence the name equity). Their denomination (par value) is fixed at 25p, 50p, £1, etc. and their market price is usually quoted in pence. Their dividend (return) is the last call on company profits; high profits enable high dividends to be paid and vice versa. In addition, high profits can cause a rise in the share's price, producing a capital gain for shareholders. The dividend payable is determined by the directors who are unlikely to distribute all the profits, retaining some to finance future growth. Because the effectiveness of the management determines dividends and share prices all ordinary shareholders possess full voting rights, usually one vote per share. A non-voting 'A' share is an ordinary share without voting rights but these are now uncommon and many firms have commuted them into ordinary equities. On a company's liquidation the ordinary shareholders share the net assets once other creditors have been paid.

Share prices
These are affected by: (*a*) company's performance; (*b*) rumours; (*c*) general state of the national economy; (*d*) speculators; (*e*) inflation.

(*a*) *The company's performance.*   If investors accept a P/E ratio of 12 an improvement in company profits that causes the P/E ratio to fall would allow the share price to rise to restore a P/E ratio of 12.

Example:

Earnings	6p per share	share price 72p	P/E 12	(72 ÷ 6)
Earnings	8p per share	share price 72p	P/E 9	(72 ÷ 8)

Therefore share price rises to 96p to restore P/E ratio to 12 (96 ÷ 8).

Any factor improving profitability will therefore have a beneficial effect on the share price and vice versa.

Indicate the effect the following events would have on the shares listed below (*a*)–(*f*).
1. A revolution in an African country with numerous copper mines.
2. A 25 per cent rise in petrol prices.
3. A 20 per cent devaluation of the peseta.
4. The resignation of the whole board of XYZ.
5. A miners' strike.
6. The development of cheap calculators.

The shares of
(*a*) a tour operator dealing exclusively with Spain	Fall/Rise
(*b*) a copper-mining company with no mines in the African country	Fall/Rise
(*c*) a motor car company	Fall/Rise
(*d*) XYZ share	Fall/Rise
(*e*) a company producing log-burning stoves	Fall/Rise
(*f*) a company producing adding-machines	Fall/Rise

(See answers, page 75.)

(*b*) *Rumours.*   Suggestions of possible mergers or take-over bids will affect share prices.

(*c*) *The general state of the economy.*   This, unlike (*a*), affects all share prices. Trade union acceptance of pay policy may cause share prices to rise and an adverse balance of payments will have the opposite effect. The Stock Exchange is also highly sensitive to political events such as a change of Government.

(*d*) *Speculators.*   Investors anticipating a fall in a share's price will sell shares they do not possess hoping to purchase them at a lower price before the end of the account to be able to satisfy the first bargain on settlement day.

Example:
sell   12,000 shares in XYZ on 2 October for 74p.
purchase   12,000 shares in XYZ on 11 October for 70p.

The speculator's profit is 12,000 × 4p (less expenses). This speculator is a 'bear'. Investors expecting a price rise will buy shares to sell before the end of the account at a profit. This speculator is a 'bull'. The influence of speculators is marginal compared with factors (*a*) and (*b*).

(e) *Inflation.*   Share prices will automatically rise to compensate for inflation. If all other factors are equal an inflation rate of 10 per cent would result in share prices rising by 10 per cent.

The small investor lacking specialised knowledge or wishing to spread the risk by investing in numerous small companies may purchase shares in a unit trust. The unit trusts specialise in different areas: some attempt to maximise capital appreciation, others seek a high yield or specialise in foreign securities. The unit investor entrusts funds to the investment manager in return for units in the trust. The

Table 11.1   Stock Exchange quotation

1979 High	1979 Low	Stock	Closing price	+ or −	Dividend (%)	Yield (%)
160	70	Smiths Group (50p)	160	+10	5	15.6
240	220	Brown's Corpn (£1)	227 xd	− 2	16	7.0
27¹/₂	16¹/₂	Jones Photographic (5p)	16¹/₂	− 3¹/₂	8	2.4
58	46	Greens Industrial (10p)	58	+ 4	14	2.4
£17¹/₈	£16¹/₂	Roberts Bros (£5)	£17	—	12	3.5
(a)	(b)	(c)	(d)	(e)	(f)	(g)

F.T. Index 560 (h)

Column:
(a) The highest price the stock has achieved since 1 January in the current year.
(b) The lowest price the stock has achieved since 1 January in the current year.
(c) The name of the stock with its nominal value.
(d) The closing price at the end of the previous day's trading. The term xd ('ex dividend') signifies that the dividend recently declared will be paid to the seller and not any purchaser of the share. Where the words 'cum dividend' are used the purchaser of the share is entitled to the dividend.
(e) This indicates the increase or decrease on the previous day's price.
(f) This is the percentage dividend based on the share's nominal value. Brown's have declared a 16 per cent dividend which means each share receives 16p (16 per cent of the par value £1).
(g) An investor is interested in the return available on shares purchased at their current price. The last column indicates the percentage return based on the market price and is calculated by the following formula.

$$\frac{\text{Nominal value} \times \text{Dividend}}{\text{Market price}} = \text{Yield}$$

The higher the share price the lower the yield and vice versa.
(h) The Financial Times Industrial Ordinary Share Index (F.T. Index). This is used to measure the movement of share prices and comprises 30 shares, each of which is a recognised market leader. An increase signifies a rise in general share prices and vice versa.

individual possesses no right of ownership over the fund's individual investments, only in the fund, the share price of his units reflecting the value of the shares held by the trust. Each unit trust has a trustee who ensures it is administered for the shareholders' benefit.

The advantages of a unit trust for the small investor are:

1. The management of her share portfolio is conducted by the unit's investment managers.
2. A small investment can be spread over many securities, thereby spreading risks.
3. The trust can be chosen because it fulfils her investment criteria.

Investors monitor their shares' progress from the financial pages of newspapers who publish an abridged version of the 'official list' of the Stock Exchange. This contains a full description of each quoted security stating in various columns the relevant information for the investor. Table 11.1 illustrates the main points.

2. Companies

The Stock Exchange enables industry to raise its long-term capital from investors. Industry requires permanent funds whilst investors may wish to liquidate their investments, their shares must be marketable. By providing a market for the sale of second-hand shares the Stock Exchange reconciles these two opposed objectives. A company obtaining additional capital by issuing new shares or debentures would use the new-issues market. Although the two markets are distinct they are interdependent and could not exist without each other.

3. Institutions

These are now the most important investors. Large institutions such as insurance companies, pension funds and banks may possess surplus funds which can be invested for short or long periods. Whilst retaining liquidity the money earns interest, enabling the institutions to provide better facilities for their customers.

4. Government

The Stock Exchange enables the Government to borrow large sums of money at favourable rates of interest through the sale of gilt-edge securities. In addition the gilt-edge market can be used as part of the Government's economic policy.

Glossary of terms

Account: a period of two successive weeks during which dealings are put together for settlement on account day.

Account day/settlement day: the day on which all bargains struck during the account are settled. It is usually a Tuesday, seven working days after the end of the account.

Bear: investor who sells securities which he does not possess in the hope of repurchasing them at a lower price.

Bear market: falling market (i.e. share prices are falling).

Broker: an intermediary between parties to a business transaction.

Bull: an investor who buys stock in the hope of reselling it at a higher price.

Bull market: rising market.

Cum dividend: price of share includes right of the buyer to receive dividend or interest shortly to be paid.

Debenture: a security issued by a company against a loan which is secured on its assets.

Dividend: payment of profits to shareholders.

Ex dividend: if the share is sold, seller retains right to dividend shortly to be paid.

Gilt-edge: UK-guaranteed stocks.

Jobber: a person who makes a market in stocks and shares. She acts as a principal and may only act with brokers and other jobbers.

Jobber's turn: difference between price at which she buys and sells securities.

Nominal value: par or face value of a share or bond.

P/E ratio: multiple of last published earnings per share represented by current price.

Yield: $\dfrac{\text{Nominal value} \times \text{dividend}}{\text{Market price}}$

Answers

(*a*) rise; (*b*) rise; (*c*) fall; (*d*) fall; (*e*) rise; (*f*) fall.

Examination questions

1. Is a rise in the Financial Times Share Index favourable to the investor? Briefly explain your answer.

(*Q. 1(c)   1977*)

2. In which financial institution would you find a bull, a bear, and a stag?

(*Q. 1(j)   1976*)

3. Below are some Stock Exchange statistics for 18 November 1975.

1975 High	Low	Stock	Price	Change
13	4½	Allied Plant	12½	
155	30	Ang. Am. Asphalt	150	−5
73½	26	Armitage Shares	62	+1
197	64	A.P. Cement	195	+7
115	47	Atlas Stone	114 xd	+2

(a) Explain precisely the meaning of each column.
(b) What is the significance of xd after the price of Atlas Stone?
(c) Give three reasons why the price of a share might rise, and three reasons why it might fall.
(d) Distinguish between a share and a debenture.

(Q. 6 1976)

4. Distinguish between 'a jobber' and 'a broker'.

(Q. 1(b) 1975)

5. Distinguish between a cumulative preference share and an ordinary share.

(Q. 1(e) 1977)

6. Distinguish between a 'yield' and a 'dividend'.

(Q. 1(j) 1978)

7. What are 'gilt-edge' securities?

(Q. 1(c) 1978)

8. Information on shares in the manner outlined below could be found in a newspaper's financial section. Answer the questions that follow it.

1973 High	Low	Stock	Price	+ or − (%)	Dividend	Yield (%)
120	57	Smiths Group (50p)	102	+13	5	2.9
258	153	Browns Corporation (£1)	200	+4	10	
31½	15½	Jones Photographic (5p)	20½	−½	22½	5.4
52	42	Greens Industrial (10p)	49xd		20	4.1
350	225	Roberts Bros. (25p)	262	+5	37½	3.7

(a) What would have been the most advantageous price for you to have bought Smiths shares in 1973?
(b) The yield (%) for Browns has been omitted. What is it?
(c) What is the nominal share value of Jones Photographic?
(d) The current price of Greens is quoted as 49xd. What does xd signify?
(e) What were yesterday's prices for Jones and Roberts?
(f) 'The dividend on Roberts shares makes them an outstanding bargain.' Support or reject this statement.
(g) Share prices fall and rise for a variety of reasons. Put forward three suggestions that could have led to Smiths putting on 13p in a day.

(Q. 4 1974)

Business insurance
Chapter 12

Insurance is a financial service which enables those suffering financial loss to be compensated. Without it risks would be borne by the individual concerned. If a business were burnt down, unless the owner could finance its rebuilding she would be forced out of business. Insurance eliminates this possibility. It is based on the principle that although numerous individuals run the same risk only a small number will actually suffer loss. If those subject to the same risk, for example fire, each pay a small sum, this creates a pool from which those whose properties are destroyed can be compensated.

Payments in	Pool	Compensation
$10,000 \times £10$ $= £100,000$	$\rightarrow \quad £100,000 \quad \rightarrow$	$90 \times £1,000$ $= £90,000$

Essentials of a contract

(a) The parties
The party seeking insurance may be a private individual or business. Whilst negotiating for the policy the customer is called the **proposer**, on obtaining it she becomes the **insured** or **policyholder**. The suppliers of insurance are the **underwriters** (or **insurers**). These can be public companies, such as the Prudential Insurance, Commercial Union and Legal and General, or mutual companies (owned by their policyholders and not shareholders) like Standard Life and Norwich Union. The most famous underwriters are those resident at Lloyds of London. These represent their syndicates, affecting mainly marine and aviation insurance on their behalf. Today, however, the largest insurer is the Government through the National Insurance scheme.

Although insurance contracts require only two parties, many refer to third parties. These are individuals acquiring rights under the agreement. In motor insurance policies the third party is the other person involved in any accident, for whose benefit the 'third-party insurance' is taken out.

(b) The proposal form

Everybody seeking insurance completes a proposal form. The information provided determines the premium and because only the proposer possesses all the material facts she must answer every question truthfully (she must show the **utmost good faith**). Witholding relevant information allows the contract to be set aside. In one case where a proposer innocently failed to disclose a previous criminal conviction which, had it been known, would have increased the premium, the insurance company successfully refused to pay out £30,000 fire insurance.

(c) The premium

The information provided on the proposal form enables the insurance companies' actuary to calculate the premium. This is the sum the proposer periodically pays to the insurance company. In certain policies, for example motor insurance, a policyholder not claiming on her policy receives a 'no-claims bonus' which reduces the premium.

(d) The cover note

When the premium is paid a policy is drawn up giving details of the cover. A cover note stating that the insurance has been granted is issued until the policy is ready. This is essential in motor insurance where driving without insurance constitutes a criminal offence.

(e) The policy

This document contains the terms of the contract.

(f) The renewal notice

When the premium, usually paid in advance, is due the insurer sends a renewal notice. This is accepted when the premium is paid. If the terms of the policy are altered the insurer encloses a document called an endorsement. The insured attaches this to the original policy and both documents constitute the amended contract.

Principles of insurance

(a) Insurable interest

This arises where the insured possesses a financial interest in the risk insured. Without this any insurance money received would be profit and not compensation and if X could insure Y's house against fire the temptation is obvious. A wife possesses an insurable interest in her husband's life (the death of the breadwinner involves financial loss), an owner has an insurable interest in her car, house and business, etc. Contracts of insurance where there is no insurable interest are void and ineffectual.

(b) Indemnity

Excluding life policies, the function of insurance is to indemnify (compensate) the policyholder against losses, not to allow her to make a profit. If a house is insured for £30,000 and fire causes £15,000 of damage the policyholder can recover £15,000 and not the full value of the policy. Thus over insurance, with the consequent higher premium, is worthless except as a hedge against inflation. Where a policy contains a 'subject to average' clause the insurer can only recover such proportion of her loss as the value of her property bears to the value of the insurance cover. So if it is insured for less than its real value, the whole loss, even though less than the sum insured, cannot be recovered. If B's house, worth £50,000, is insured for £25,000 and fire causes £25,000 of damage she can only recover £12,500. If a house valued at £30,000 is insured for £20,000 only two-thirds (£20,000/£30,000) of any damage is recoverable.

(c) Contribution

Contribution occurs when property is insured with more than one insurer (double insurance). If the contract is one of indemnity the insured can only recover to the extent of her loss. She can claim against one or all of the insurers but each must contribute to the loss in proportion to the amount for which they are liable under the contract. Any insurer paying more than her share can obtain a contribution from the others. If Z's house, worth £30,000, is insured by two insurers (each for £30,000) and it is totally destroyed she can only recover £30,000. If she claims £30,000 from one company, that company can obtain a contribution of £15,000 from the other. The principle is inapplicable to contracts of life insurance which are not contracts of indemnity and a person can affect insurance with numerous insurers and claim each policy in full.

(d) Subrogation

Where the insurer pays out under a policy she is entitled, by the doctrine of subrogation, to every legal and equitable right of the insured. She can pursue any remedies that would have been available to the insured. If a vehicle is written off and the insurer pays on the basis of total loss she is entitled to the vehicle and can sell it as scrap. If the damage was caused by X's negligence she can also bring a negligence action.

Types of policy

The distinction between insurance and assurance is that the latter is concerned with inevitable events: the policyholder's death or the expiration of a fixed period of time. Insurance is concerned with events that may happen: the death of a policyholder within 25 years or a motor accident.

The following outlines some of the policies that might be taken out by:

(a) The individual

Most individuals should possess life insurance. *Whole life assurance* involves the assured paying premiums until her death when her next of kin receives a lump sum. A variant on this is *term insurance* whereby the policyholder insures her life for a specified period at the conclusion of which the policy lapses.

Both types of policy provide security for the assured's family whereas an *endowment assurance*, which is payable after a set period or prior death, provides security and a lump sum after a fixed period. Although more beneficial than the other two, the premiums are higher. Any life policy 'with profits' entitles the policyholder to the nominal value of the policy plus a share of the company profits.

Motor insurance policies are a common feature in most households and as building societies make their mortgages conditional upon the property being insured against fire, fire insurance is also very common. The prudent houseowner will probably possess a comprehensive policy which protects against fire, flood, lightning, storm, etc. and loss of personal property.

(b) The business

The policies taken out will depend on the nature of the business. As almost all businessmen rent or lease property they require fire insurance to cover both premises and contents (the policy may also cover loss of business resulting from the fire), and complementing this would be a policy against burglary.

Businesses employ staff and employers *must* insure against the possibility of staff being injured due to defective equipment or premises. As employers may be liable for negligent acts committed by their employees whilst at work they may carry insurance against this possibility. A specialised type of this insurance (a fidelity guarantee policy) arises where the employee is in a position of trust which provides them with an opportunity to embezzle money. The insurance company undertakes to indemnify the employer against any sums stolen by the employee.

Where the business involves exporting, marine insurance will be required against loss or damage to the ship and goods whilst at sea.

Insurance can also be taken out with the Export Credits Guarantee Department of the Department of Trade to cover him against losses that may occur in dealing with a foreign purchaser.

Both individuals and businessmen pay into the State insurance scheme which provides medical care and pensions (although the latter is often supplemented by private schemes). Other specialist policies exist but these are too numerous to mention.

Effect of insurance on the UK economy

The insurance industry is an important contributor to invisible exports. Both Lloyds and the major insurance companies sell policies overseas, thereby helping to transform an adverse balance of trade into a favourable balance of payments. Insurance also encourages the growth and assists the survival of small firms by allowing insurance against risks which if they occurred might otherwise force firms into bankruptcy. Without it larger companies would require large cash reserves for possible emergencies but by insuring these are released for more productive purposes. The insurance industry is also the largest single institutional investor on the Stock Exchange and can provide funds for expanding or newly emergent companies. These can then provide additional employment opportunities. Apart from this indirect boost to employment the insurance industry is itself a large employer.

Examination questions

1. What do you understand by 'no-claims bonus' in an insurance contract?

(Q. 1(g)   1977)

2. Briefly explain the following terms connected with insurance:
   (a) premium;
   (b) indemnity;
   (c) policy;
   (d) endorsement;
   (e) fidelity guarantee;
   (f) underwriter.

(Q. 5   1977)

3. Why is an insurance company better able to afford risks than is a firm seeking insurance cover? Give two examples of insurance cover a firm might seek.

(Q. 4   1976)

4. What is meant by an insurable risk?

(Q. 1(h)   1975)

5. What are the main principles underlying insurance agreements?

(Q. 11   1975)

6. In motor insurance contracts who is the 'third party'?

(Q. 1(b)   1976)

7. Imagine you are an insurance agent trying to 'sell insurance' to a small business. Explain the main insurances you would recommend and the reasons why you think they are needed by this business.

(Q. 6 1978)

8. What are the chief risks that the owners of a small factory might insure against?

(Q. 10 1974)

International trade

Chapter 13

International trade arises when one country sells to, or buys from, another.

Advantages of international trade

1. It enables countries to consume products they cannot produce because of geological or climatic conditions.
2. A country such as the UK cannot be self sufficient and relies on international trade for basic commodities. Over half the food consumed is imported and most raw materials for manufacturing industries must be imported.
3. Countries can import goods they are capable of producing and concentrate their resources in other areas. They, like individuals, benefit by specialising in their most efficient areas (this is the principle of comparative costs). Specialisation increases the world's total production so all nations benefit economically.
4. It encourages international co-operation because all nations are interdependent. One nation's problems may affect other nations, hence the increasing number of 'summit' meetings where Heads of State consider the world's economic problems.
5. The UK also benefits from trade because many necessary services are provided by the 'City', which increases our invisible exports.

When unemployment is high demands are frequently made to curtail international trade. It is argued that if we stop importing (buying) items but instead produce them ourselves this would necessitate new factories, creating more jobs and thereby lowering unemployment. This argument, however, assumes that countries buying our goods will not retaliate by banning our exports. If they did, factories producing goods for export would close down, increasing unemployment.

Trade is therefore both desirable and essential. Countries must, however, balance their accounts; expenditure cannot continually exceed income. A country's accounts in international trade are called the balance of payments. Money entering Great Britain is recorded as a + (plus) and money leaving as a − (minus). A country's accounts consists of the items listed in Table 13.1.

Table 13.1

1. Goods exported	+	100
2. Goods imported	−	140
		Balance of Trade = (deficit) − 40
3. Services exported	+	80
4. Services imported	−	20
		Balance of Payments on current account (surplus) = + 20
5. Investment abroad	−	20
6. Investment in UK by foreigners	+	40
7. Foreign deposits of cash in UK	+	20
		Balance of Payments = + 60
8. Borrowing from I.M.F.	+	
9. Addition to reserves	−	60
10. Withdrawal from reserves to pay debts	+	
		Balance = NIL

Items 1 and 2 in Table 13.1 are called **visibles**, consisting of finished goods (e.g. cars, whisky, glassware) and raw materials (e.g. oil, coal). Their main characteristic is they can be seen, hence their name. Exports are a + because foreigners pay us, hence money flows in. The balance of visibles is the **balance of trade**, a deficit being called a 'trade gap'. A breakdown of the main UK export and import trade is given in Fig. 13.1. The majority of exports are manufactured, hence the Government's concern over the strength of the manufacturing sector (see Table 13.2).

Table 13.2

Exports	Percentage of total value (1978)
Food, beverages and tobacco	6.4
Basic materials	3.5
Fuels	4.7
Manufactures:	
Machinery and transport equipment	36.7
Chemicals	13.0
Metals and metal manufactures	10.4
Textiles	4.5
Other manufactures	18.4
Miscellaneous	2.4

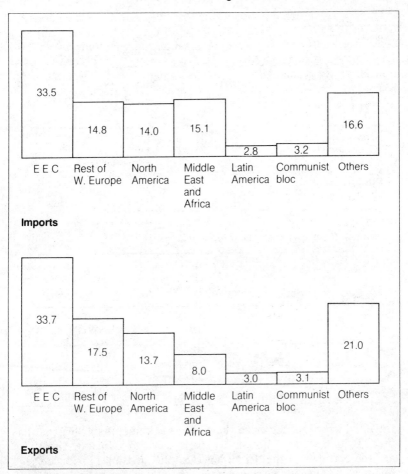

Fig. 13.1 Britain's customers

Imports indicate the recent growth of manufactured and semi-manufactured goods at the expense of raw materials, reflecting the growing industrialisation of the developing countries (see Table 13.3).

Trade also involves selling and buying services such as banking, technical advice, insurance, etc. The 'commodity' bought cannot be seen. Items 3 and 4 of Table 13.1 are therefore called **invisibles** – the UK normally exports more than it imports (see Table 13.4).

Government expenditure is primarily on the upkeep of embassies and foreign military bases and is usually in deficit. Historically shipping was a large contributor of foreign currency but the relative decline of British shipping has resulted in the current position. The largest invisible earners are interest from British investments overseas, and

Table 13.3

Imports	Percentage of total value (1978)
Food, beverages and tobacco	16.3
Fuels	20.0
Industrial materials:	
Basic materials	11.2
Chemicals	6.8
Other semi-manufactures	20.7
Finished manufactures:	
Machinery and transport equipment	16.9
Other manufactures	7.2
Miscellaneous	0.9

Table 13.4 (Students to fill in most recent information)

	Invisible exports (£m.)			Invisible imports (£m.)		
	1971	1976	197	1971	1976	197
Government	57	215		584	969	
Shipping	1,588	3,251		1,657	3,206	
Interest, profits, dividends	1,440	4,832		940	2,567	
Travel	469	1,628		443	1,008	
Civil aviation	354	1,051		310	810	
Others	1,292	2,861		462	3,112	
Surplus				804	2,166	

travel which benefited from the fall in the value of sterling that has made Britain a 'cheap' holiday for overseas visitors. Included in others are the earnings of the 'City'. Visibles plus invisibles produce the **balance of payments on current account** which can be in surplus (exports exceed imports) or deficit.

Money transactions are not all in payment for goods and services. Foreigners invest in British companies, and UK residents and companies invest overseas. If investment in the UK exceeds investment abroad this provides a surplus to offset any deficit in the balance of payments on current account. It is a short-term solution as foreign investors eventually require repayment. Item 7 of Table 13.1 is similar to item 5, except foreign funds are not invested in companies but deposited in banks to earn interest. This 'hot money' swells our reserves until the foreigners decide to invest it elsewhere.

Items 1–7 of Table 13.1 make up the balance of payments which will be a surplus (+) or deficit (−). A deficit can be financed by:

(*a*) Borrowing from the International Monetary Fund (see below). As money flows into the country it is a + (item 8, Table 13.1).

(*b*) Selling gold or foreign currency from our reserves; selling gold means an inflow of currency and so is a + (item 10, Table 13.1)

A surplus allows an increase in reserves. We purchase gold or foreign currency and as payment is in sterling it is a − (item 9, Table 13.1).

The financial position of countries A, B. C and D can be calculated from the following figures (£m):

	A	B	C	D
Goods exported	100	90	90	100
Investment abroad	60	20	20	30
Services imported	30	80	40	60
Foreign deposits of cash in UK	20	100	30	10
Goods imported	90	100	160	130
Services exported	50	60	60	100
Investment in UK by foreigners	30	10	20	30
Addition to reserves				
Withdrawal from reserves or Loans from I.M.F.				

Country A possesses a healthy surplus on both balance of trade and payments. Country B has a deficit on balance of payments on current account but can add to reserves. This appears healthy but the £100m lent by foreigners (allowing reserves to rise by £60m) could be withdrawn. If this happens the reserves fall by £100m (£40m more than the increase). Country B is living today but will receive the bill tomorrow. Country C's balance of trade deficit of £70m is not balanced by the small invisible surplus or inflow of foreign funds. This results in borrowing or depletion of reserves. Country D is in a satisfactory position. A visible trade deficit is compensated by an invisible surplus producing a favourable balance of payments on current account. Favourable capital movements permit an additional increase in reserves.

A country must eventually equate expenditure (imports) with income (exports) and a balance-of-payments problem can be solved in numerous ways: 1. reducing imports; 2. increasing exports; 3. borrowing.

1. Reducing imports

If domestic industry becomes more efficient, people will 'buy British', thereby reducing the import bill. Certain commodities must be imported but the UK imports items such as televisions, cameras, washing machines, etc. which it also produces itself. The UK both imports (Table 13.5) and exports cars.

Table 13.5 Imports of cars (£m.) (Students to fill in most recent information)

1974	669
1975	910
1976	1,432
1977	2,133
197	

If foreign goods cannot be home-produced, imports can be reduced by:

(a) Tariffs

This is a tax on imported goods; a 10 per cent tariff increases the price of a £3,000 car by £300 (10 per cent of £3,000). The higher price should reduce demand and hence the level of imports. The defect of tariffs is that they reduce demand by increasing prices, which creates inflation.

(b) Quotas

This method does not raise prices. It involves setting a limit on the number of items imported. If 5,000 cars per month are imported, a monthly quota of 2,500 would halve imports. Both tariffs and quotas must be agreed with the other EEC countries. Whilst tariffs and quotas may improve the balance of payments they can also:

1. Protect infant industries. When an industry is starting it cannot compete with established industries with advantages of economies of scale. A trade barrier protects the infant industry until it has grown sufficiently strong.

2. Stop dumping. This involves a foreign producer selling in this country at below cost price ('dumping goods').
   This can be profitable.

Example:
Cost of producing 200 typewriters: £100 each.
Sells on his home market for £110.
Profit 200 × £10 = £2,000
Cost of producing 400 typewriters: £90 each (lower cost due to economies of scale).
200 sold on his home market for £110
Profit 200 × £20 = £4,000
200 'dumped abroad' for £85 each.
Loss 200 × £5 = £1,000
Net profit £4,000 − £1,000 = £3,000

To obtain economies of scale, production must increase. The extra machines cannot be sold at home, they must be exported. To achieve this they sell below cost. The additional profit obtained on the home market compensates for the losses incurred in dumping.

3. Raise revenue.

(c) Exchange control
This final method of reducing imports only allows foreign currency to be spent on certain commodities. As purchases cannot be made without foreign currency this restricts imports of other items.

2. Increasing exports

Exports are increased when home products become more competitive. Apart from improving the product, a lower price improves competitiveness. Even without a price reduction the price the foreigner pays falls if the value of sterling falls. The *value of sterling* reflects its exchange rate with other currencies, for example, the Malaysian dollar. If £1 obtains five dollars, a fall in the value of sterling means it buys fewer dollars, say four. Our goods immediately become cheaper for Malaysians whilst imported Malaysian goods become more expensive.

Example:
English shirt sells at £8
Exchange rate £1 = 5 Malaysian dollars
Cost of shirt to Malaysian = 40 dollars (exchanged to obtain £8)
Exchange rate £1 = 4 dollars
Cost of shirt to Malaysian = 32 dollars (exchanged to obtain £8)

Example:
Malaysian shirt sells at 50 Malaysian dollars
Exchange rate £1 = 5 dollars
Cost of shirt to Englishman = £10
Exchange rate £1 = 6 dollars
Cost of shirt to Englishman = £8.33

In the second example above, sterling's value has risen against the dollar (it buys more dollars) so making Malaysian goods cheaper to the Englishman, and vice versa.

Example:
Malaysian shirt sells at 35 Malaysian dollars
Exchange rate £1 = 5 dollars
Cost of shirt to Englishman = £7
Exchange rate £1 = 4 dollars
Cost of shirt to Englishman = £8.75

In the above example the pound has fallen in value making the Malaysian shirt more costly. A fall in the value of the pound makes British goods cheaper to foreigners and their goods more expensive to import. (A rise produces the opposite effect.) If the lower prices encourage exports and the higher prices discourage imports the balance of payments will improve. The 'falling pound' does not always benefit the balance of payments. The next example considers the exchange rate of sterling with the US dollar.

Example:
Exchange rate £1 = 2 US dollars
UK imports 100 tons of wheat at $10 per ton
Cost = £500 ($1,000)
but

Value of £ falls to £1 = $1
UK imports the same quantity of wheat at $10 per ton
Cost £1,000 ($1,000)

If imports remain constant they cost more if the pound falls. This increases the import bill. Many imports are raw materials that are imported regardless of cost (e.g. oil) and the falling pound increases their cost. Consequently shop prices rise, worsening inflation. Conversely, lower prices may not increase sales sufficiently to compensate for the lower price. Foreigners may not buy British cars because they break down frequently and spare parts are unavailable. There may be 'invisible' tariffs; these are unseen barriers which make exporting difficult. The Government may set high safety standards for imported items which change frequently, making it difficult for firms to comply. Numerous import regulations may exist, making it difficult to keep delivery dates.

If a government uses a falling currency to improve the balance of payments the right conditions must exist, otherwise it causes inflation and a deteriorating balance of payments.

Exports can also be encouraged by the Government providing free or cheap credit for exporters or by the negotiation of trade deals. Under these the other country agrees to purchase certain goods in return for trade concessions.

3. Borrowing

A country whose expenditure exceeds its income must borrow; one lender is the International Monetary Fund (I.M.F.). This was created in 1944 to secure international monetary co-operation in important matters. It lends to member countries to finance short-term balance-of-payments deficits. This provides 'breathing' space whilst the imbalance is corrected.

Inflation and the balance of payments

Although these topics may appear unconnected there is a close relationship.

Example:
Cost of car in UK £3,000
Cost of car in France 30,000 francs
Exchange rate £1 = 10 francs
Inflation in UK 10%
Inflation in France 5%
Cost of UK car £3,000 + £300 = £3,300
Cost of French car 30,000 francs + 1,500 francs = 31,500 francs if exchange rate remains the same
French car sells in UK for £3,150 (31,500 ÷ 10)
English car sells in France for £3,300
Hence UK citizens find French cars cheaper, therefore imports rise but French citizens find UK cars more expensive, and so exports fall.
Result: deteriorating balance of payments.

This results in an increased demand for foreign currency to pay for imports and a declining demand for sterling. This causes a fall in the value of the pound, making exports cheaper and imports more expensive which causes higher prices.

Foreign exchange markets

These are necessary to exchange currencies so an English importer can for example obtain the francs to pay his French supplier. The London Foreign Exchange Market consists of Authorised Banks and Finance Houses plus Foreign Exchange Brokers, each specialising in a foreign currency, who act as intermediaries between buyers and sellers. Brokers cannot deal on their own account and their rates of commission are fixed by the Brokers' Association. The market is controlled by the London Foreign Exchange Bankers' Committee assisted by a committee of the London Foreign Exchange Brokers' Association.

The exchange rates quoted can be divided into:

1. Those for immediate exchange of currency ('spot' or 'cable' rate). If B is exchanging travellers' cheques for francs or obtaining francs from her English bank for her holiday this is the rate in which she will be interested.
2. Those for the 'forward exchange' of currency. An Englishman, C, might purchase French perfume with payment in three months' time. To ascertain the UK selling price he must know the rate of exchange he will obtain when the date for payment arrives. By purchasing 'forward' the bank will tell him the rate they will give him in three months' time; if the franc is 'hardening' (becoming more valuable) this will be below the 'spot' rate and vice versa. A manufacturer receiving payment in dollars in three months' time can also settle the rate he will receive at that time. The forward rate is quoted as a 'premium' or 'discount' on the spot rate.

Fluctuations in exchange rates occur when changes occur in the balance of payments. A deficit causes the value of sterling to fall because the demand for foreign currencies rises to pay for increased imports whilst the demand for sterling falls (fewer foreigners require sterling to pay for exports). A surplus has the opposite effect. Sterling's value is also affected by interest rates; if they are higher in London than other financial centres this causes an influx of capital and an increased demand for sterling. To avoid continually fluctuating exchange rates, which would be detrimental to trade, the Bank of England attempts to offset the movement of 'hot' money. When changes in exchange rates become likely, however, speculators will buy and sell currency to take advantage of the changes. If an Englishman buys £100 of francs when the rate is £1 = 10 francs he receives 1,000 francs. If the rate improves to £1 = 8 francs he can sell the francs for £125. Ignoring commission his profit is £25.

Examination questions

1. Explain, giving examples, the term **invisible exports**; could there be **invisible imports**?
   (Q. 8   1972)

2. Why is the North Sea so important for the United Kingdom?
   (Q. 1(c)   1974)

3. What is the difference between 'visible' and 'invisible' trade?
   (Q. 1(j)   1974)

4. Examine the main advantages to be derived from international trade.
   (Q. 5   1974)

5. Is money spent by an American tourist in London, UK, a British import or a British export? Briefly explain your reasoning.
   (Q. 1(a)   1976)

6. What is the difference between a quota and a tariff?
   (Q. 1(c)   1976)

7. 'The pound has fallen against the American dollar.' Does this make our exports cheaper for Americans to buy, or more expensive? Briefly explain.
   (Q. 1(a)   1977)

8. 'Although the balance of trade is in deficit the overall balance of payments is favourable.' Briefly explain how this could be so.
   (Q. 1(b)   1977)

9. Give a simple explanation of why 'gold and foreign currency' reserves are so important to the value of a nation's currency.
   (Q. 1(h)   1978)

10. What precisely is meant by the 'Trade Gap'?
    (Q. 1(i)   1978)

11. Discuss **four** ways in which an adverse balance of payments may be corrected.
    (Q. 2   1978)

12. Why may it pay a country to import goods which it can produce itself?
    (Q. 3   1978)

European Economic Community

Chapter 14

This was formed on 25 March 1957 when representatives of France, Germany, Italy, the Netherlands, Belgium and Luxembourg ('the Six') signed the Treaty of Rome. Further countries have joined the original six, Britain and the Irish Republic becoming members on 1 January 1973.

The Treaty established a common market by eliminating tariffs between member countries, thereby creating the world's largest trading group; the population of EEC countries exceeding 250 million. As the Community develops it is hoped to establish a joint economic policy producing continual economic expansion for member countries. In addition, a closer political union is envisaged between members. Ultimately this should result in a Western European political union able to play an important role in world affairs. Few developments have taken place in this sphere but member countries have adopted common policies on certain aspects of foreign policy.

Community institutions

1. The Assembly

More commonly called the European Parliament, this consists of 142 members who since 1979 have been elected by direct universal suffrage. Its role is mainly deliberative, acting as a forum for expressing views on Community policies. It possesses the power to dismiss the Commission (requiring a two-thirds majority) which means the Commission must appear before the Parliament to explain its policies.

2. The Council

This body, which usually meets in Brussels, consists of one minister from each member state, normally the Foreign Minister (each is

Chairman for a six-month period). When matters other than foreign policy are discussed the relevant specialist minister can attend, for example, when food prices are considered the Ministers for Agriculture are present. The Council considers the Commission's proposals which it rejects or accepts; it cannot modify them or initiate its own proposals. Major Council decisions must be unanimous and so any minister believing proposals are harmful to his country can veto them (as did France in the late 1960s). Once the Commission's proposals are accepted they take legal effect.

3. The Commission

This is the most important EEC institution, consisting of 13 members (2 from Germany, France, Italy and the United Kingdom and 1 from other member countries) appointed for four years by unanimous agreement of the member governments. It possesses a staff exceeding 10,000 and is partially independent financially, receiving the income from the Community's external tariffs. The Commissioners act as individuals and not as representatives of their countries (being specifically prohibited from receiving instructions from their governments) which ensures the Commission is supra-national, putting Community before national interests. Each Commissioner is responsible for the running of a department within the Commission. It initiates proposals and is the executive body for implementing Community programmes. Commission decisions are by a majority *but* a meeting is only valid if all members are present. Who are the British Commissioners?

The EEC and Britain

1. Businesses

The main advantages for the British businessman stem from the Community's customs policy. A protective wall of common customs duties (Common External Tariff) surrounds the EEC to restrict imports of non-EEC countries whilst within the Community there is free movement of goods. Tariffs (visible and invisible) and quotas have been eliminated between member countries and no member state can unilaterally reimpose trade restrictions. If this becomes necessary to safeguard the balance of payments the other members' consent must be obtained prior to their imposition. This means UK businessmen have direct access to a market exceeding 250 million (approximately five times the UK market). Because of the rules ensuring fair competition they can compete equally with foreign businessmen: selling in EEC countries is almost as easy as selling across county borders. The increased sales potential makes possible increased production with economies of scale thereby increasing our competitiveness. The removal of British trade barriers against Community countries means, however, greater competition for UK businessmen in the domestic market.

The fair-competition rules (briefly mentioned above) attempt to ensure the most efficient location of industry within the Community. The ideal situation involves each country producing those items where it is most efficient, hence maximising the advantages of international trade. If governments 'assisted' inefficient industries to survive, this would limit the advantages of international trade; therefore aid-distorting competition is prohibited (although state aid for disaster or backward areas is permitted). The Commission constantly reviews all systems of state aid and its approval is required in each case.

2. Labour

The Community permits free movement of persons, making it easier for Britons to work abroad. As most workers cannot emigrate, the existence of the European Social Fund is probably more important. This was established 'to help ensure the re-employment of workers who have to change their jobs in member states as a result of technological developments in industry and the effects of economic integration and greater competition.' Any country retraining or resettling staff obtains 50 per cent of the cost from the fund. This benefits countries, like the UK, possessing retraining programmes.

3. Housewives

The housewife should benefit because the Community seeks to provide:

  (i) a greater range of commodities at lower prices;
  (ii) greater price stability, especially in food;
  (iii) continuity of supplies. In 1975 there existed a world sugar shortage; the Common Agricultural Policy (CAP) should ensure that a future world shortage does not effect the EEC housewife.

These objectives are long-term and the necessary policies may initially result in higher prices, as exist in food. The methods adopted to achieve (ii) and (iii) are illustrated by examining the CAP.

(a) Stabilisation of food prices

Changes result from fluctuations in supplies. Bumper harvests cause falling prices; poor harvests cause them to rise. The Community policy is for the FEOGA (European Agricultural Guidance and Guarantee Fund) to purchase surpluses to avoid prices falling and release these at times of shortage. The price at which the Fund purchases food from the producers is the **intervention price**, which is fixed by the Commission. This is a guaranteed minimum price and once market prices fall below this figure the farmer sells his produce at the intervention price to the FEOGA.

(b) Continuity of supplies

To ensure EEC food production can meet the demands of the European housewife (i.e. make the Community self-sufficient) it is necessary to stimulate food production. This is also essential to achieve price stability. The inefficient European agricultural industry of the 1960s meant considerable food imports with prices fluctuating with the state of world harvests. The Community attempts to encourage production by:

1. Grants to farmers who adopt more efficient methods.
2. Provision of training facilities.
3. 'Pensions' to encourage inefficient farmers to vacate the land in favour of more go-ahead producers.
4. A high intervention price (higher than prevailing world prices). This stimulates production by guaranteeing farmers a high price for their products. As efficiency improves, intervention prices will equate with world prices and even if they remain slightly higher this is a reasonable price to pay for self-sufficiency and stable prices.

To restrict imports of cheap foreign food, at below the intervention prices, there is an import levy bringing prices up to EEC prices, for example:

World price	EEC price	Import levy
10	14	4
7	12	5

If world prices exceed EEC prices, European farmers would export food to obtain the higher prices. To restrict this, farmers exporting pay an export levy which is roughly equal to the difference between the EEC and world market price. This reduces the financial incentive to export, for example:

World price	EEC price	Export levy
14	12	2
16	13	3
14	9	5

The policy necessary to ensure certainty of food supplies will lead to high prices but the European housewife pays unnecessarily high prices for certain commodities. Because of political pressures some intervention prices (those for dairy produce and cereals) are too high, encouraging overproduction (because it is very profitable for farmers) and surpluses. These are purchased by the FEOGA and the artificially high price ensures overproduction in following years and increases in the Community surplus. This produces the:

butter mountain	1976 store	260,000 tonnes
wine lake	1976 store	370,000,000 galls
skimmed milk desert	1976 store	1,100,000 tonnes (5½ years' supply)

To reduce surpluses the EEC often sells the products to non-EEC countries at below the intervention price, for example:

market price for butter	70p
price given to farmers by FEOGA	80p
sold to USSR	60p

Estimated cost in 1976 to subsidise the production of surpluses, store them and sell some at a loss was £2,000 million (i.e. £8 for each person in the EEC).

Surpluses could be reduced by lowering 'intervention prices', thereby discouraging production. Lower prices would also encourage consumption but the reduction in farmers' incomes is politically unacceptable. The situation is politically sensitive because countries with large agricultural industries (France) seek high intervention prices whilst countries with less dependence on agriculture (Germany) prefer lower prices.

4. Law

To ensure the Community becomes a more fully integrated unit each member must, in Community matters, ensure its laws correspond to those existing in the EEC. British decisions could, in a few cases, be overruled by the Court of Justice in Luxembourg (on which a British judge sits) but the majority of English Law is unaffected by our membership of the EEC.

Examination questions

1. Name two of the main institutions of the EEC.
   (Q. 1(j)   1976);

2. Discuss the EEC demonstrating how the course you have taken has given you a better understanding of the issues involved.
   (Q. 11   1978)

3. Briefly explain the relevance of the words 'Common' and 'Market' as applied to the EEC.
   (Q. 1(a)   1973)

Economic systems
Chapter 15

The central problems of an economy

No country possesses sufficient resources to produce all the goods and
services it would like. Hence a country's economic system must
develop a mechanism for solving **three** fundamental economic
problems:

What goods and services should a country produce?	Because resources required for production are scarce the decision on 'what to produce?' also determines 'what cannot be produced?'
How should these goods and services be produced?	An economic system, having decided what will be produced, must decide the most efficient methods of producing the goods and services.
How should the output of goods and services be shared by society?	As there are insufficient goods and services it is necessary to determine the share going to individual members of society.

Different economic systems

Different countries and different societies have answered these
fundamental economic problems in different ways. The **two**
hypothetical extremes are:

Free enterprise   _____   Planned
economy   economy

1. The free-enterprise economy

In this economy the three central problems – what to produce; how to produce it; and how society shares the output – are determined by individual choices as reflected by the **price mechanism**. The price of a product or service depends on public demand and its supply. If there is a fall in demand and supply remains unaltered there will be a fall in price.

Example:
Apples demanded at 20p/lb.   400 lb.
Demand falls to 200 lb.
Therefore:
(*a*) 200 lb unsold
(*b*) Retailers, unable to sell, lower prices to avoid being left with bad apples.

Manufacturers make less profit and some will switch their resources into producing commodities in greater demand, with higher prices, where profits are higher. Consumers' demand therefore determines the goods and services produced.

Example:
(*a*) Apple prices fall due to falling demand.
(*b*) Farmers obtain lower prices for their apples.
(*c*) Pear prices are high because of higher demand.
(*d*) Farmers switch production from apples to pears to take advantage of higher price.

A similar mechanism determines 'how the goods will be produced'. The most efficient manufacturers have the lowest costs of production and therefore the lowest prices. Consumers will purchase the cheapest items forcing the less efficient producers with higher prices into liquidation. Hence the most efficient methods of production are used.

In the free-enterprise system an individual's share of the total output depends on her purchasing power (income). This depends on income from property and her wages and salary, which is determined by the 'price mechanism'. An increased demand for a particular skill causes the price paid (wages) for the skill to rise. The demand for a particular skill, or type of labour, depends on the demand for the product that type of labour produces. Hence the purchasing decisions of individual consumers indirectly affects wages.

Example:
(*a*) 100 craftsman thatching cottages for £100/week.
(*b*) Thatching becomes popular and demand trebles, causing a two-year waiting list.
(*c*) Customers unwilling to wait offer £200/week to encourage thatchers to work for them.
(*d*) Higher wages for thatchers.

In a free-enterprise economy the **price mechanism** decides *what* will be produced, *how* it will be produced, and *how* it is to be shared. There would be no government intervention that interfered with individuals' choice, which determines the answer to the three economic problems.

In practice a complete **free-enterprise system** does not exist since it possesses considerable disadvantages, which are considered below.

(*a*) *Collectively provided services*
Some services such as law and order and national defence can only be provided effectively on a national scale, which means government

involvement. Many nationally provided services (education, health, etc.) are considered fundamental to society and so must be available to everybody. It is possible that under a free-enterprise system only the very rich could afford them and so government intervention is again essential.

Government intervention may also be necessary to provide services that individuals would not demand but which are essential in any civilised society. Libraries, public conveniences, parks and museums would probably not be provided under a completely free-enterprise system but without them our quality of life would suffer.

(b) The 'pull of purchasing power'
Because the production of goods and services responds to the pull of purchasing power, industrialists would cater for the demands of the wealthy (e.g. by producing luxury goods) often at the expense of the basic needs of the poor.

(c) Monopoly power
Free competition is essential for the free-enterprise system to operate. The growth of monopolistic companies causes a distortion in the allocation of resources. A greater demand for their products should produce an increase in production but the monopolist may not increase production, thereby keeping his prices (and his profits) artificially high. By stopping the free movement of resources he frustrates the wishes of the consumer.

Combinations of employees have a similar effect. When demand for a product falls causing a reduction in the demand for labour this should result in lower wages, thereby encouraging workers to move to other occupations. Because unions stop wages falling and workers being made redundant, the operation of the free-enterprise system is frustrated.

In modern economies numerous large firms and unions possess monopoly powers which distort the operation of the price mechanism (see Table 15.1).

(d) Social costs
Under a free-enterprise system the 'profit motive' is paramount and firms may ignore the social implications of their actions, such as pollution of the environment. A firm may discharge chemical waste into a river because this is the cheapest method of disposal, ignoring the effects on fishing and swimming.

(e) Unemployment
Because demand depends on the whim of consumers, the demand pattern will alter if consumers' tastes change, or fall if there is a temporary reduction in purchasing power. The first causes a change in the structure of industry; firms whose products have lost their popularity will close whilst other firms will grow. As workers are not

Table 15.1

Market	Controlled by	Union	Number of members (1978)
Sugar	Tate and Lyle British Sugar Corporation	Transport and General Workers Union	1,929,834
Soap-powder	Unilever Proctor and Gamble	Amalgamated Union of Engineering Workers	1,168,990

immediately transferable this leads to structural unemployment.
Where there is a general slackening of demand this causes a slump and
resulting unemployment (called cyclical employment).

(f) Economic growth
A key element in achieving economic growth is investment in capital
equipment (factories and machines). If individuals choose to spend
money on present consumption rather than saving it, goods will be
produced for present consumption and there will be little investment;
this will retard the rate of growth (see Table 15.2).

Table 15.2

Country	Rate of investment p.a. 1970–1975 (expressed as a % of GNP)	Growth rate p.a. 1967–1977 (expressed as a % of GNP)
United Kingdom	1.9%	1.8
W. Germany	2.4	3.8
Japan	33.3	7.6
USA	17.5	2.9

(*Source*: OECD National Accounts)

2. The planned economy

The theoretical alternative to the free-enterprise economy is the
centrally planned economy. Decisions – about: what to produce; how
to produce it; and each individual's share of the output – are
determined by a central planning authority under governmental
direction. Such a system is often called a '**command economy**',
emphasising that individual free choice is removed and resources are
allocated according to social as well as economic objectives.

This system is characterised by State ownership of the methods of
production (factories and machinery). Although the planned economy
allocates resources to reflect the needs of society, it does have
disadvantages:

(a) Bureaucracy

To make the economic decisions the central planning authority requires a considerable workforce to collect statistics and economic intelligence. These employees are engaged in non-productive work and the 'red tape' they generate can make decision-making a slow and expensive process.

(b) Efficiency

The efficient allocation of resources depends on the efficiency of the central planning authority and they may be no more efficient in judging what society requires, and what is good for society, than the collective decisions of individuals.

(c) Loss of freedom

Because decisions are made centrally the individual's freedom of choice is reduced. An individual cannot choose her brand of make-up: the central planning authority decides which one is best and she must purchase it or go without.

(c) Lack of incentive

Where the State controls the economy, personal initiative may be removed. A successful entrepreneur in private enterprise obtains wealth and power. In a controlled economy these incentives are lacking, which may discourage a potential entrepreneur from making the sacrifices necessary to succeed.

No country adopts either system in its pure form. Countries in the Eastern bloc are closer to the concept of the planned economy whilst countries in the Western bloc identify with a modified free-enterprise system.

State interference and the mixed economy

An intermediate position between these two extremes is the **mixed economy** where some decisions are taken by individuals and businesses in the private sector whilst others are taken by Government and local authorities in the public sector. The growing interference of the State in an otherwise free-enterprise system is to remedy or minimise the deficiencies outlined above.

Sample questions

1. What is meant by the term '**mixed economy**'?
2. Services such as health, education, and defence are provided either by Central Government or by Local Authorities. What problems would occur if their provision were left entirely to the private sector of the economy?

State influence in the UK economy

Chapter 16

Main areas of Government expenditure

The main feature of UK Government expenditure has been its growth, expressed as a percentage of Gross National Product. In 1900 it was 12 per cent; 1910, 12 per cent; 1951, 40 per cent; and in 1978 it exceeded 50 per cent. This is primarily due to increasing expenditure on social services, such as pensions, social security, health and education and the growing State intervention in the economy which is reflected in the growing numbers of civil servants. Figure 16.1 indicates the different areas of Government expenditure.

There has been a proportionately decreasing expenditure on defence (1900, 26 per cent; 1951, 25 per cent; 1968, 14 per cent), despite the expensive nature of modern technological welfare, and on repayment of the National Debt (1932, 25 per cent; 1951, 11 per cent; 1961, 10 per cent).

Main sources of revenue

The most important sources are:

1. Taxation

Functions of taxation
(a) Raising the revenue for Government expenditure.
(b) Achieving social objectives such as the redistribution of income; products causing pollution can also be taxed so the 'social costs of pollution' are borne by the manufacturers and consumers.
(c) Restricting consumption of undesirable products: 'saving consumers from themselves'.
(d) Protecting industries from foreign competition.
(e) Helping the Government achieve its economic objectives ('fiscal policy').

10.8	Defence
13.7	Education
23.7	Social security
16.9	Social Services
3.1	Law and order
7.7	Housing
4.2	Roads
2.8	Overseas Aid
4.7	Trade and Industry
9.0	Miscellaneous
3.4	National debt repayment

Fig. 16.1 How each £1 is spent

Quantities of a good tax
The ideal tax should be related 'to the ability to pay'. Whether this means **proportional** (everybody paying the same percentages in taxes), or **regressive** (the rate of tax paid declining as incomes rise) or **progressive** (the rate increasing as income rises) is debatable, but probably progressive taxes are best related to the individual's ability to pay. Income tax in the UK is a progressive tax (see Table 16.1).

Fairness also dictates that taxes should be certain (taxpayers knowing how much to pay and when) and impartial (equally affecting individuals with the same income). Because of their revenue-earning function their costs of collection must be as low as possible. An ideal tax should therefore be convenient to pay and economical to collect. Where a tax possesses social objectives it might be acceptable even though expensive to collect, providing it achieves these objectives. As fiscal policy is becoming increasingly important, an ideal tax should be capable of being quickly and cheaply altered should this become economically desirable.

Table 16.1 Income tax table

1979–80 Band (£)	Rate (%)
1–750	25
751–10,000	30
10,001–12,000	40
12,001–15,000	45
15,001–20,000	50
20,001–25,000	55
over 25,000	60

Direct taxes
These are collected by the Inland Revenue and are levied on income.
Examples of direct taxes are income tax, corporation tax, capital gains
tax, wealth tax and a gifts tax. In the UK income tax is the most
important source of revenue.

The advantages of direct taxes are:

(a) Although they can be regressive or proportional they are usually
     progressive, unlike indirect taxes.
(b) Their effective incidence is easily determined because the person
     paying also suffers the tax.
(c) They are less inflationary than indirect taxes which increase
     prices.

The main disadvantages are:

(a) Progressive direct taxes are probably a disincentive to effort. A
     progressive tax falls most heavily on 'marginal' income (i.e. the
     last income earned) because additional income is taxed at a higher
     rate than previous income. At the highest income levels if additional
     income is almost all paid in tax there is little financial gain
     which lowers the incentive to work. The disincentive
     effect is probably most pronounced at higher income levels.
     Inflation has made UK taxes more progressive in recent years as
     the levels at which higher rates of tax begin have not kept pace
     with inflation. It has been argued that because a progressive tax
     reduces income the taxpayer has to work harder to achieve the net
     income necessary to maintain her standard of living. It is certain,
     however, that the steeply progressive tax system has resulted in
     the emigration of many better-paid employees (the 'brain
     drain').
(b) Progressive direct taxes encourage the growth of non-taxable
     perks, avoidance and evasion.
(c) Progressive taxation also reduces the occupational and
     geographical mobility of labour. Promotion requires effort and
     possibly training and where financial rewards are eroded by

taxation, individuals may be unwilling to make the necessary sacrifices. Moving to a new area is costly and if the extra salary is eroded by tax the move may be economically pointless.

(d) Progressive taxes may reduce the division of labour. If X earns £10 per hour but loses 80 per cent in tax his net income is £2 per hour. If a garage charges £5 per hour it pays X to repair his own car, even if this takes him twice as long as the skilled mechanic. Sacrificing two hours' work costs him £20 in lost salary but his net loss is £4 and the garage bill would be £5: he is £1 better off. One pound unspent, being tax free, is worth more than £1 earnt.

(e) Progressive taxes reduce the capacity to save and may deprive the wealthy of their savings. This reduces the level of investment with economically undesirable consequences.

(f) Progressive taxation may deter enterprise. A small-businessman unable to write off losses against profits may be unwilling to commence a new venture. There is no compensation for bankruptcy whilst most of his profits will be paid in tax.

(g) A company tax penalising distributed profits, whilst encouraging investment in that firm, will reduce funds (by reducing shareholders' income) available for investment in new and perhaps more profitable companies. This is economically undesirable.

Indirect taxes (outlay taxes)
These are collected by Customs and Excise and are levied on expenditure (outlay). Examples are customs duties and VAT.
  The advantages of indirect taxes are:

(a) Even if they are progressive (which is unlikely) they have less disincentive effect than direct taxes with equivalent progression. The effect on the taxpayer is identical but a direct tax affects the pay packet, whereas the taxpayer is probably unaware of the tax element in the price of a commodity. The psychological effect of each tax is different.

(b) Simple outlay taxes are easier and cheaper to collect than direct taxes.

(c) They can be used to discourage socially undesirable consumption.

(d) They can ensure a product's price reflects the 'social costs' of production. A higher rate of VAT on car exhausts that cause pollution means the costs of preventing pollution are borne by the consumer.

(e) Taxes on commodities with inelastic demands (i.e. goods whose demand remains constant despite price increases) such as cigarettes and alcohol allow the estimated revenue to be accurately estimated.

(f) They are better instruments of fiscal policy because they can be quickly changed and have an immediate effect on demand, an

increase reducing the amount of money available for consumption and vice versa.
(*g*) They are publicly more acceptable, not affecting the pay packet.
(*h*) If the progressiveness in the tax system needs to be reduced, a reduction in the progressiveness of direct taxes would meet political opposition but a switch from direct to indirect taxes will reduce progressiveness in an unobtrusive way and is therefore politically more acceptable.

The disadvantages of indirect taxes are:

(*a*) They are usually regressive although progressiveness could be achieved if items purchased by the wealthy were taxed at a higher rate. This is difficult since the best commodities to tax are usually essentials, because they possess inelastic demands. It is difficult to relate indirect taxes to the ability to pay.
(*b*) They are not impartial, the consumers of inelastic products (cigarettes and alcohol) being heavily penalised.
(*c*) They are inflationary. They increase prices, the Retail Prices Index rises, causing higher wage demands which, if met, cause higher prices, leading to an inflationary spiral.

Overtaxation may have economically undesirable consequences. Britain's 'taxable capacity' (the proportion of the Gross National Product taken in taxes) has risen from: 10 per cent in 1913; 20 per cent in 1925; to over 40 per cent in 1978—see Fig. 16.2. This level of taxation, it is claimed, lowers a country's rate of growth by reducing the supply of labour and capital (above) whilst encouraging inflation. Because company profits are highly taxed, increased costs are more acceptable because they are mainly borne by the Inland Revenue (the higher cost reducing taxable profits). High wage demands, encouraged by high indirect taxation, are therefore more likely to be accepted, causing an inflationary spiral.

2. Borrowing (National debt)

The debt is still mainly owed to British citizens but the Second World War and successive balance-of-payments crises in the 1960s caused a rise in borrowings from foreign governments and this latter debt has serious economic implications. Interest and capital repayments have to be paid for by exports. This produces pressure on the balance of payments as the loans in the 1960s were not used to increase productive capacity but to finance a country living beyond its means. The interest payable depends on the size of the debt and interest rates: the lower the rate the lower the repayments. Although the debt has increased its real cost is less today than in 1920.

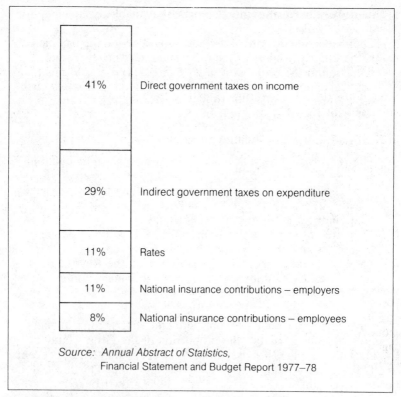

Fig. 16.2 Composition of text burden (1977–78)

Main aims of Government economic policy

Firstly, an important Government objective is the attainment of full employment. This means an unemployment rate of below 2.5 per cent (some workers being unemployable). Secondly, this must be linked with a reasonable rate of economic growth, this being the only way to achieve a real rise in living standards. Thirdly, both must be achieved without inflation as rising prices produce an arbitrary redistribution of income (causing hardship to groups on fixed incomes) and balance of payments problems. The fourth objective is to obtain an equilibrium in the balance of payments. A major problem is that full employment and economic growth require rising prices. If these rise too fast the balance of payments goes into deficit, necessitating restrictions on economic activity, and this produces unemployment and declining economic growth. Successive British Governments have been unable to sustain economic growth because of recurring balance-of-payments crises.

Main methods of economic control

1. Fiscal policy

The use of taxation as a tool of economic policy commenced in 1947. During slump conditions (unemployment, static production and limited investment) Government expenditure will exceed revenue (budget deficit) and in inflationary periods there will be a budget surplus. The latter decreases the amount of purchasing power in the economy, which checks demand and reduces the inflationary pressure. Although taxes may be varied by 'mini-budgets', major tax changes are usually announced in the Budget. The Chancellor presents this to the House of Commons in late March or early April of each year. He describes economic progress since the last Budget and explains his policy for the forthcoming year, giving estimated expenditure and outlining proposals for obtaining the necessary revenue.

2. Monetary policy

Money is not merely a medium of exchange. Its supply (amount) and cost (interest at which it can be borrowed) affects the size of the national income, employment, savings and investment. The State's monetary policy is therefore of great importance. To understand how this controls the supply of money, the role of bank deposits in the monetary system must be appreciated. Over 80 per cent of money transactions involve bank deposits and only a small proportion of these were created by customers depositing money. Most deposits were created by banks through lending. The banks' power to lend is therefore important in determining the volume of 'money' in the economy.

If ten customers deposit £1,000 a simplified bank-balance sheet would be:

Liabilities	Assets
Customer deposits £10,000	Cash in hand £10,000

Most transactions are conducted by cheque and only a small percentage of deposits are withdrawn in cash. If cash withdrawals are 10 per cent of total deposits the bank only requires £1,000 cash in hand (10,000 ÷ 10). Cash assets of £10,000 would be sufficient for deposits of £100,000. The bank can therefore lend £90,000 (by creating or increasing existing bank deposits) to customers, producing the following balance sheet:

Liabilities	Assets	
Customer deposits £100,000	Cash	£ 10,000
	Money owed by customers	£ 90,000
£100,000		£100,000

The amount the banks can lend is therefore determined by the percentage of deposits they must hold in cash. If this is 20 per cent of original deposits they can only lend five times the original deposit. The 'Minimum Reserve Ratio' (MRR) is the amount of cash (and other liquid assets) they must hold and is fixed by the Bank of England (currently 12.5 per cent). If central Government wishes to increase lending (the supply of money) they will, via the Bank of England, lower the MRR and vice versa.

Money borrowed also depends on interest rates and the Bank of England 'Minimum Lending Rate' (MLR) determines all interest rates. An increase in the MLR causes a rise in rates and vice versa. The above are the direct controls affecting the supply of money (bank loans and advances) and the price (interest rates) but the Government, through the Bank of England, also controls these by indirect means. In a submission to the EEC the Bank of England said, 'The information regularly supplied by the banks forms the basis for interviews at which recommendations are made to those banks, any aspect of whose general conduct . . . is not . . . altogether satisfactory . . . Such requests and recommendations are in practice effectively mandatory, and no bank wishing to continue to operate in the London market would refuse to comply.'

3. Other controls

(a) Hire-purchase
Variations in the deposit required or the repayment period can affect economic activity, a decrease in the deposit or an extension on the repayment period stimulating consumer spending. The use of these controls can create uncertainty in industries dependant on hire-purchase, which may delay investment plans and produce other undesirable side-effects.

(b) Legislation
This ranges from controls over prices, profits and wages to the provision of incentives encouraging desirable forms of economic activity such as persuading firms to set up or expand in areas of high unemployment (called 'Areas for Expansion' [AE]). The Industry Act (1972) and the Local Employment Act (1972) provide grants for new

machinery or building schemes and assistance towards the cost of transferring 'key' workers. These are employees required to install plant or machinery, train local employees, or provide the nucleus of the workforce; employees can obtain assistance towards fares, a settling-up grant, temporary separation allowances and assistance with the sale and purchase of property. Employers providing jobs for unemployed workers receive loans at favourable rates and a grant of up to 80 per cent of the costs of moving to the AE (which includes any redundancy payments made); in addition the Training Services Division provide their services free (usually there is a charge). These services include providing instructors to help train new and existing employees and the use of 'training within industry' facilities to develop skills in instruction and communication, handling staff problems and improving work methods. Where training in instructional skills is required, Instructor Training Courses are available.

In addition to incentives the government can 'persuade' firms to move to the AE. Where tenders for public contracts are equal, Government departments, nationalised industries and other public bodies must favour firms in AEs and following an unsuccessful tender they may re-tender for up to 25 per cent of the original contract. Industrial development requires an Industrial Development Certificate but these are dispensed with in areas of high employment. An application may also be refused if the firm could operate in an area of high unemployment.

(c) *Public spending*
Through the spending of nationalised industries and Government departments pressure can be applied to industry. In 1977 and 1978 firms breaking the Government's voluntary pay policy were placed on a 'black-list' and not awarded Government contracts. This policy was short-lived however and at the end of 1978 the Government withdrew the use of sanctions against firms breaking their pay policy. In addition, by varying public expenditure the Government can influence the level of economic activity.

(d) *National Enterprise Board (see pp. 43 and 60)*

National Economic Development Council

This body is an important institution in the economic relationship between Government, unions and management. It comprises representatives of all three groups, is chaired by the Prime Minister and it possesses sub-committees considering special economic problems. It considers economic issues and advises the Government on appropriate policies.

Examination questions

1. The Government controls the economy in a variety of ways. Distinguish by examples between fiscal and monetary policy.

   (Q. 1(i) 1977)

2. Give: (i) **one** example of a direct tax; and
   (ii) **one** example of an indirect tax.

   (Q. 1(d) 1976)

3. Name a reason (other than the raising of Government revenue) why tax is levied.

   (Q. 1(c) 1975)

4. Explain briefly the main purpose of the annual Budget presented to Parliament.

   (Q. 1(b) 1978)

5. Select a number of examples to demonstrate the growing influence of the State in the economy and the community.

   (Q. 10 1978)

6. What fundamental objectives does a Government set out to achieve by imposing taxes?

   (Q. 11 1973)

Technology and change

Chapter 17

'Science and technology have come to pervade every aspect of our lives and, as a result, society is changing at a speed which is quite unprecedented. There is a great technological explosion around us, generated by science.' (Sir Leon Bagrit)

It is impossible to discuss recent changes in technology and new materials because by the time of publication these will be outdated. We have therefore considered the impact of technology so students can understand technological changes that occur.

The firm

The product of modern technology, automation, is the logical successor to mechanisation. It covers every conceivable activity, commercial, governmental and social, and affects everybody. The computer, the centre of any automated system, works at phenomenal speeds – measured in nanoseconds (a thousandth of a millionth part of a second) – which enables decisions to be based on up-to-date information. The manufacture of commodities as different as ice-cream and steel are now computer-controlled.

By raising productivity automation lowers production costs and hence the final price. Any manufacturer failing to introduce automation therefore risks being priced out of the market. The growth of the computer chip ('mini-computer') enabled digital watches to replace ordinary watches (causing unemployment in the Swiss watch industry) and the pocket calculator to replace the desk adding machine. The mini-computer possesses applications outside business. Programmes are being prepared so that semi-trained medical staff can feed in patients' symptoms to a computer, conduct tests as instructed by the computer and finally receive the diagnosis with the course of treatment. By programming the computer with the latest information, every patient will benefit from the most recent research.

The cost of computer hardware (the computer) has fallen and the main cost of installing a computer is often the program (software). This only has to be written once and therefore after an initial capital outlay the running costs are relatively low.

Case study: Word processor
A typist's productivity is related to the number of mistakes she makes. Time is spent correcting these and a serious mistake can necessitate a document being retyped. The word processer eliminates typing mistakes, thereby increasing productivity. The processor possesses a type keyboard with a television screen (video display unit). The letter, document, etc. being typed is shown on the screen and mistakes are remedied by pressing the appropriate key. When the video text is complete it is printed (at 500 w.p.m.) by the electronic printer. In addition letters can be stored on magnetic cards and produced simply by inserting these into the memory bank. If a standard letter (or document) requires minor alterations only the amendments need typing. Documents can therefore be updated without the need for complete retyping. The unit (based on the computer chip) raises productivity and reduces much of the drudgery of office life, but eliminates the need for copy typists.

The employees

Modern industrial systems possess a strong technological bias necessitating heavy capital expenditure. To ensure the effective use of technology, accurate planning is essential, hence the elimination of variable factors is encouraged. This leads to unemployment amongst 'blue collar' workers because machines are more certain than labour; they do not strike or demand higher wages. Basic manipulative tasks are being performed by machines at the expense of the skilled and semi-skilled workers. Automation also requires fewer 'blue collar' workers because its technology can only be operated by those 'educationally' qualified, excluding skilled workers who lack the correct educational background. That automation achieves higher production with fewer workers is not disputed. The largest single private employer in the United Kingdom (G.E.C.) reduced its labour force from 230,000 to 180,000 between 1969 and 1972 whilst profits rose from 49 to 72 million pounds over this period.

Hence increased production will be achieved with fewer workers but the greater wealth generated will increase demand for service industries, which will therefore employ larger numbers. The transference of employment from agriculture and manufacturing to service industries is a feature of most industrialised societies.

One method of minimising automation's effect on employment levels would be the introduction of a shorter working week combined with a shorter working life, perhaps commencing at the age of 25 with retirement at 50. The increased leisure time would, it is assumed, be welcomed by the employee who could earn enough money by working perhaps only three days a week. American experience over the last 30 years has questioned this assumption. Since 1940 the average working week in industry has remained constant despite the introduction of a shorter working week because of the increasing amounts of overtime worked. It is argued that man's wants will never be satisfied – new needs will be created by advertising – so that he will always seek more money to satisfy these wants.

How will the worker employed in automated industries fare? Many of the dull routine tasks will be eliminated but whether the remaining jobs will be as enjoyable as before automation is arguable. Those in favour of automation assert that by providing better information a computer will allow a manager to manage better, utilising his capabilities to the full. The analogy has been drawn of a man with a telescope; by using a telescope (computer) he can see further (manage better) and if he wishes to see further (manage better) he must be provided with more complex equipment (a more advanced computer). Opponents of automation claim that it eliminates decision-making, and the majority of employees perform boring, dull and uninteresting jobs. Failsafe and other safety devices minimise the operator's role, eliminating his sense of responsibility and creating frustrations. As one opponent has claimed, 'automation seems to disconnect men from the machines . . . Mass production having disposed from man the creative forms of work, he becomes dispossessed by automation of the control over his work.' Even if the work is more enjoyable it will be organised to meet the demands of the computer rather than vice versa: an idle computer loses money. Because of the employment issues, union reaction to new technology will determine its effect on industry.

Technology, unemployment and underdeveloped countries

Technology has already caused unemployment in these countries by causing the population explosion in the last 30 years. World population is growing by 2 per cent per annum; by the year 2010 it will have risen to 7.8 billion from 3.9 billion in 1975, most of this increase being in underdeveloped countries. The major cause is the falling death rate caused by technological advances in medicine. For example, the elimination of the malaria mosquito in Sri Lanka halved the death rate between 1945 and 1954 (a decline that took Europe over 100 years to achieve). Because agricultural land is fixed the additional workers migrate to cities, putting further pressures on their inadequate services, thereby creating sprawling urban slums. Calcutta has a slum of 7 millions (1977) with an estimated population of 60 million in the year 2000!

The feeding of the extra millions will pose problems for the West. In addition, because of the vast quantities of raw materials imported from these countries (see Table 17.1) the West will be concerned with their political stability.

Table 17.1

	Domestic production consumed by underdeveloped countries	Exported
Petroleum	24.6	75.4
Coal	103.00	−3.00
Iron ore	17.00	83.00
Bauxite	25.00	75.00
Copper	10.00	90.00
Lead	37.5	62.5
Zinc	36.2	63.8
Nickel	4.00	96.00
Tin	10.7	89.3

Political instability might arise because:

1. Technology is widening the gap between the rich and poor nations, the latter being unable to invest in the new technology.
2. Technology is creating 'two nations' within the underdeveloped countries. The vast numbers of agrarian workers are very poor whilst employees in automated factories are well paid, forming a small privileged elite. The benefits of technology accrue to a small percentage of the population.

Society

A major stimulus to industrial change will probably arise from society's response to the new technology. Technology has enabled world production to rise at 7 per cent per annum with a corresponding increase in the demand for natural non-renewable resources. Between 1900 and 1950 consumption of mineral resources exceeded the world's entire consumption before 1900 and since 1950 it has increased by 50 per cent. In 1970 gold deposits were expected to last until 1979, silver 1983, tin 1985 and zinc 1988. There will therefore be pressure on industry to develop technology which:

1. Enables better utilisation of existing resources. The world's oil reserves were increased by technology permitting underwater exploitation. New technology may enable ore with such a low mineral content (which at present is useless) to be utilised. Aluminium initially required pure ore (without silica and iron) but

new technology permitted impure ore to be used. This meant reserves doubled between 1950 and 1958.
2. Permits substitute materials to be used, e.g. substitution of aluminium for copper, synthetic fibres for natural products.
3. Permits recycling of waste products. At present 40 per cent of US lead consumption, 30 per cent of iron, 22 per cent of copper and 11 per cent of aluminium is met by recycling scrap. Tin cans cannot be recycled because of the inner coating of tin but if this were replaced by a resin, recycling would be possible.

All the above will require energy, a non-renewable natural resource. An industrial priority must therefore be the discovery of an acceptable new source of energy. Solar energy might be the answer but at present it would require a solar 'panel' with an area of 15 square miles to supply power for a town of one million inhabitants. Nuclear energy, a possible panacea, has to overcome the problem of nuclear wastes – isotopes – which are dangerous to humans for possibly hundreds of thousands of years. Where will they be stored? This was the problem discussed at the Windscale Enquiry of 1978.

As consumption of raw materials rises they will become scarcer and more expensive, which will be a calatyst for industrial change. Western industry has already experienced rising oil prices.

Manufacturing activities automatically produce waste. Technology, by increasing production, increases the pollution problem. Natural disposal systems such as rivers, oceans and air are inadequate to dispose of man-made waste. The air is polluted by car exhaust fumes, rivers by industrial waste, and oceans by sewage and oil. Increased concern over pollution centres around:

1. The nature of modern waste. It is often so complex that its effects cannot be diagnosed and the dangers may be realised too late (e.g. the dangers of working with asbestos).
2. The possible damage to the ecosphere (the system that supports life on earth). This involves a delicate balance between air, heat, water, etc. and if pollution upsets this delicate balance our planet may be unable to support life. There has been concern over the emission of gases used in aerosol cans (previously considered harmless) which may have damaged the ozone layer which filters out harmful ultraviolet radiation from the sun's rays.
3. The immediate destruction of life by pollutants. Fertilisers are washed into rivers where they remove oxygen from the water, with disastrous effects on the aquatic life (several years ago large numbers of fish died in the river Rhine). In Minamata in Japan over 100 people suffered from food poisoning after eating fish in which mercury had become concentrated. Swimming can become dangerous due to sewage disposal, one well-known sea being so polluted it is called the 'black lagoon'.

Governmental concern has produced legislation such as the UK Clean Air Acts which reduced deaths from air pollution (see Table 17.2) and the Control of Pollution Act (1974).

Table 17.2

Year	Central London Smoke (p.p.m.)	SO₂ (p.p.m.)	Deaths due to pollution
1952	6,000	3,500	4,000
1962	3,000	3,500	750
1972	200	1,200	nil

It is now a criminal offence to deposit toxic wastes on private tips. Legislation may therefore force industry to change.

Pressure groups are attempting to force industry to adopt techniques producing less waste but so far industrialists have caused pollution with impunity because of the principle of 'externality of costs'. The cost of cleaning up pollution is not borne by the industrialist and, not being a cost of production, is excluded in the final price. The person paying is not the consumer but the individual who suffers from the pollution, even though she does not consume the product. When making production decisions, firms can ignore the costs involved with pollution. If Government action required manufacturers to pay the costs of eliminating pollution this would then become a cost of production and be passed on to the consumer by means of higher prices. If car exhausts which cost more but emitted a lower level of lead content were compulsory, the cost of de-polluting the atmosphere would be borne by the car-users who are partly responsible for its pollution.

Unless all these problems are solved, the world could run out of natural resources or become too polluted to sustain life. Technology may, however, be able to extend the 'day of reckoning' almost indefinitely. Plant varieties, for example, are being developed which require virtually no fertilisers.

Alternative technology

Groups exist who believe that survival will necessitate a change in the technological base of society and industry, the adoption of so-called alternative technology. This would involve industry accepting the following new principles:

1. Production of goods that are easily recycled.
2. Production of lasting products, as opposed to the current practice where 'the problem is to make our products obsolete before someone or something else does'.

3. Production should require the minimum use of scarce resources.
4. Production methods should produce the minimum amount of waste matter.

Even these changes would be insufficient for some groups whose solutions involve a radical change in the Western way of life, with the emphasis on less sophisticated technology and greater harmony with nature. The ideal society according to R. Clarke would be 'a countryside dotted with windmills and solar houses, studded with intensively but organically worked plots of land, food production systems dependent on the integration of many different species with timber, fish, animals and plants playing mutually dependent roles; with wilderness areas plentifully available . . . a life-style for men and women which involved hard physical work but not over-excessively long hours or in a tediously repetitive way.'

Monitoring the business environment

Chapter 18

This book has attempted to give the reader a background understanding of the business world. Such an understanding must be supplemented by an intelligent observation of the current business issues and economic events through reports in the press and television. Consider the following news headlines:

'Sterling at highest level against the dollar for nearly a year.'
'Prime Minister pleads at T.U.C. Congress for further wage restraint.'
'Financial Times Index breaks magic 500 barrier.'
'Minimum lending rate leaps $2\frac{1}{2}$%'.
'Unemployment reaches 1.45 million – a post-1945 record.'

Some of these reflect events which occur at regular intervals (e.g. T.U.C. Annual Congress), whilst others occur irregularly and as a response to a particular situation. This chapter deals with some key indicators and events which are worthy of further study through the press and television.

Four economic issues form the backcloth to most economic and business decisions and the underlying economic policy of the Government. They are: Inflation; Unemployment; Balance of payments; and Economic growth. The current position in these areas can be ascertained by examining certain key indicators.

Inflation

Inflation may be defined as a significant and sustained rise in prices which causes a corresponding fall in the value (or purchasing power) of money. In Britain one of the main indicators which monitors the rise in prices is the 'Retail Price Index.' This stood at 100 in 1974 (base year) and by August 1978 had reached 199.4 which means that over this period prices had almost doubled (99.4 per cent increase). One pound in 1974 purchased almost twice as much as it did in 1978. Published monthly, the Index is widely quoted in the media and indicates the success or otherwise in the battle against inflation. It is often quoted as a percentage increase over a given time period, e.g. 'April 1977 to April 1978 showed a 7.9 per cent increase in the Retail Price Index'.

Unemployment

Unemployment is a serious and continuing problem with accompanying business, political and social implications. It may be monitored through monthly figures which show the total numbers unemployed and the percentage of the population unemployed.

Example:
September 1978   1,378,100 unemployed, which is
                      5.8 per cent of the workforce

Balance of payments

The chapter on 'International trade' (Chapter 13) stressed the need to export and remain competitive. The reader should keep up to date by monitoring the balance-of-payments figures which are published monthly, with more detailed figures available on a quarterly basis. The publication of these statistics has a profound effect on business confidence and the reader should note how they cause repercussions in other areas of the business world, such as exchange rates and stock exchange indices.

Production output and growth

Since we cannot sell and export unless we produce, a key factor in understanding the current business situation is to know whether our output of goods and services is increasing. The statistic which records this figure is known as Gross Domestic Product at **Factor cost**. This stood at 100 in 1975 and by the first quarter of 1978 had reached 106.2, rising to 108.2 in the second quarter.

Figures relating solely to industrial production are produced monthly and are based on 1975 = 100.

	1978	
	June	*July*
Industrial production	111.4	111.8

It is necessary to treat these figures with caution with allowances being made for inflation, population changes, hours of work, etc. but they provide a reasonable guide to the rate of growth of a nation. Although all these statistics can be monitored through the general media they are collected together in a small monthly publication by the UK Treasury, *Economic Progress Report*, under the heading 'Monthly Economic Assessment'. This is a useful source for the recommended Economic and Business Diary to be found at the end of this chapter (Fig. 18.1).

The Budget

This occurs each April and sets the terms for the Government's economic policy.

Banking and finance

Key events to watch for include alterations by the Bank of England in the **Minimum Lending Rate** (MLR). This is one of the weapons of monetary policy and affects the interest-rate structure throughout the financial system. Note the effect an increase has on: (*a*) commercial banks (cost of loans and overdrafts); and (*b*) building societies (cost of mortgages and interest paid to depositors). When changes in the MLR occur, publicity is usually given to the meetings of the Building Societies' Association where decisions to change interest rates are made. Changes in hire-purchase controls, minimum deposits and repayment periods are also elements in Government policy. Raising the level of minimum deposit and/or reducing the repayment time makes hire-purchase less attractive and this helps deflate consumer demand.

The Stock Exchange

The Financial Times Share Index, which is quoted daily, reflects the general health of business and industry. Note changes in the Index as a response to various factors, e.g. publication of unfavourable trade figures, budget announcements and industrial action. The response of individual company share prices to particular situations should also be noted.

Business enterprise

Be aware of significant mergers, private companies turning public, companies declared bankrupt, and look for the involvement of the Monopolies Commission or the Office of Fair Trading. Each year public companies issue their Annual Report which reviews trading for the previous year and the prospects for the future. Try to read a copy of an Annual Report.

Monitor the progress of the nationalised sector of business, paying particular attention to its Annual Review (covering investment programmes and finance) each Spring and scrutinise the press for other Government involvement in industry through major subsidisation programmes, e.g. development of the Ford plant at Bridgend, South Wales, or major investment stakes in companies through the National Enterprise Board.

Training

The Government involvement is through the Training Services Division of the Manpower Services Commission. Watch out for policy statements which influence the allocation of funds and the different emphasis placed on types of training.

Industrial relations

In addition to keeping abreast of specific issues including major industrial action, crucial pay negotiations and productivity deals, students should occasionally read the *Department of Employment Gazette* which provides general statistics and articles on current issues of importance in industrial relations. Look out for the annual conferences of major trade unions and the annual meeting held in September each year of the Trades Union Congress. Monitor also the annual meeting of the Confederation of British Industry to assess the feelings of employers to main economic issues. The C.B.I. also publishes quarterly *'Industrial Trends'* which interprets current statistics and forecasts future trends in output, exports and investment.

Monthly business diary

A useful method of monitoring and keeping abreast of current business issues is to keep a small diary containing some of the key indicators mentioned in this chapter, together with some of the most important business events of the month with some comment as to relationships between the various factors (see Fig. 18.1).

Examination questions

1. Discuss what you consider to have been the most important issue, related to business, that you have read about since starting this course.

(Q. 4 1977)

2. Select any topic that you have studied on this course and show how the knowledge you gained gave you a better understanding of an item of business news which has recently occurred.

(Q. 11   1976)

3. Discuss a major news item reported in the press recently which you feel will have significant effects on your country's industry and commerce.

(Q. 8   1975)

Fig. 18.1   Business diary

	Month A
Monthly rise in Retail Price Index *Comment*: 3rd monthly rise. MLR increased as result. Substantial wage claim from main unions.	10.3 per cent
Unemployment per cent rise or fall *Comment*: Slight fall but Government measures likely to damp demand for consumer goods. Little prospect of sizeable reduction in figures.	−0.3 per cent 1,473,100
Current Balance. Balance of payments *Comment*: Despite significant revenues from North Sea oil, seamen's strike reduced level of visible exports.	−137
Industrial production 1975 = 100 *Comment*:	120
Minimum Lending Rate *Comment*: Increase in response to 3rd monthly increase in rate of inflation.	+1 per cent to 10.5 per cent
Financial Times Share Index *Comment*: Seamen's strike + 3rd monthly increase in rate of inflation. Loss of confidence. Drop from 520 of last month. Increase in MLR and tighter H.P. controls may have moderated fall.	−7 to 513
Main business events	T.U.C. Annual Congress. Seamen's Strike. Mini-budget. H.P. controls.

Special notes:
Clear from T.U.C. Annual Congress that unions will not co-operate on Government wages restraint. Loss of exports through seamen's strike. Increase in inflation rate into double figures. Tighter H.P. controls.
Indications are that period of restraint is ahead. Business less than optimistic about the months ahead.

Index